LET US ALL

EAT CAKE

LET US ALL
EAT CAKE

GLUTEN-FREE RECIPES
for everyone's favorite cakes

CATHERINE RUEHLE

with **SARAH SCHEFFEL**

Photography by Erin Kunkel

TEN SPEED PRESS
Berkeley

I dedicate this book to the memory of my father,
William Ruehle. Everything that I value most in myself
I owe to his lessons in integrity, loyalty, hard work,
and honesty. His example has always been, and will
continue to be, my gold standard.

—C.R.

CONTENTS

———

4 PLATED SLICES & LITTLE CAKES

5 DECORATED SPECIAL-OCCASION CAKES

6 ESSENTIAL FROSTINGS, FILLINGS & GLAZES

7 TIPS, TRICKS & DECORATING TECHNIQUES

INTRODUCTION

"A party without cake is just a meeting."

—JULIA CHILD

Cakes have the power to elevate an otherwise ordinary moment into something truly extraordinary. They are at the center of life's celebrations, from birthdays and weddings to graduations, anniversaries, and baby showers. We cheer up our friends by baking cakes, reward ourselves with cupcakes, and invite our children to lick frosting off the beaters. So what happens when you or your child can't enjoy that slice of cake because you can't eat gluten? I can tell you from firsthand experience.

When a Pastry Chef
Has to Give Up Gluten

For the past twenty years working as a professional pastry chef and cake artist, I've piped enough buttercream to stretch from Washington, D.C., to my hometown of Fort Worth, Texas, drizzled enough chocolate ganache to float a boat, and sifted a mountain of flour that would be a challenge for even a seasoned climber to scale. My first restaurant boss and mentor, Chef Michel Nischan, gave me the big break that turned a self-taught baker into a bona fide pastry chef. Creating cakes and pastries under Chef Nischan's direction was exhilarating, and it was clear at age twenty-five that I had found my calling; the *New York Times* raved about my desserts, calling them "breathtaking in both artistry and taste."

From there, I worked in turn as a caterer, restaurant manager, and cake designer, creating custom cakes for weddings, birthdays, and other gala events, and opened Sublime Bakery, a retail bakery and cake studio in Fort Worth. From its inception, Sublime stood at the forefront of custom cakes, incorporating organic ingredients before they were mainstream and championing gluten-free, vegan, and sugar-free baked goods before they became trendy. It came to be known as the place to turn to if your kiddo had a laundry list of allergies; we would always find a way to make a cake or cupcakes for them.

My dearest Sublime memory is of a sweet little boy named Jack; he was four when he first came in with his mom and his big brother, Pete. Pete explained that Jack had never had a "real" cupcake from a bakery because of his numerous food allergies and intolerances. Jack's mom had heard that we baked cupcakes that were gluten free and vegan, so they had come to check it out. Jack's eyes grew huge when I handed him a chocolate cupcake straight from our pastry case. This was a totally new experience for him; in the past, he'd always had to do without when the family got treats at a bakery. But he didn't hesitate for a

second—he just dived right in, face first. His joy was as pure as anything I've ever witnessed.

Little did I know that I, too, would soon need to eliminate all gluten from my diet. It happened when I was a contestant on the *Food Network Challenge,* where I quickly became known as the contestant who always goes big: on the wedding cake show, I created one of the tallest cakes in *Food Network Challenge* history—seven feet three inches tall, to be exact. But during my fourth appearance, in the midst of preparing yet another big cake—a five-foot-tall *Tyrannosaurus rex* cake—I experienced a painful tingling and paralysis in my hands. I was simply unable to complete my cake before the competition buzzer went off. The diagnosis: rheumatoid arthritis. Doctors prescribed a lifelong regime of toxic medications and painkillers, but I did my own research and, through trial and error, created a program for myself to heal my body and control the debilitating symptoms—which included eliminating food triggers like dairy, refined sugar, and, yes, gluten from my diet. Soon after, I enrolled in the Institute for Integrative Nutrition, where I became certified as a wellness coach so I could help others suffering from chronic illnesses.

My diagnosis—and the miraculous relief that the elimination of gluten and dairy provided—inspired me to develop gluten-free (and dairy-free) versions of all my favorite cakes. My goal was to create cakes and cupcakes that would be every bit as good as the originals.

So I invite you, and everyone you know with gluten sensitivities or food allergies, to grab a fork and a slice of cake and dig in with gusto. Because we all deserve to have our cake—and eat it, too! I hope you'll enjoy baking, decorating, and eating my gluten-free cakes as much as I've enjoyed creating them.

How to Use This Book

Whether you have experience baking gluten-free cakes or gluten-free baking still feels like a foreign language in need of a translator, "Your Gluten-Free Baking Pantry" (page 188) will teach you about all the ingredients you need to bake cakes that are 100 percent gluten free—and so good no one will know they're gluten free unless you tell them. Here, you'll navigate the ins and outs of selecting not only gluten-free products, but organic, all-natural, and allergen-free ingredients, too; learn how to ready your pantry and fridge for baking with an overview of high-quality gluten-free ingredients; and learn about the kitchen tools you need for superb gluten-free baking.

Then it's time to get baking. Chapter 1 is a cozy collection of simple cakes that are all a cinch to whip up in a Bundt, tube, loaf, or single-layer pan. The classic layer cakes in chapter 2 boast outrageously good frosting and cake combos, not to mention the perfect buttercream-to-cake ratios. Whether you choose to make soul-satisfying classics like Southern Coconut Cake (page 51) or German Chocolate Cake (page 55), or creative twists like my Pink Velvet Strawberry Cake (page 52), I've provided instructions for creating either traditional two-layer or towering four-layer cakes. The choice is up to you. And because we're all just crazy for cupcakes, chapter 3 is a baker's dozen worth of decadent recipes that will make any cupcake lover swoon.

When you're entertaining, you'll want to serve a cake that's as showstopping as the appetizers and entrée that precede it. In chapter 4, I pave the way with recipes for gorgeous plated cakes that are guaranteed to wow your guests. My recipes for mini cakes allow you to present every lucky guest with his or her own lavish individual dessert—from cake to dazzling garnish.

As a grand finale, in chapter 5 I share a selection of truly swoon-worthy cakes you can bake to celebrate life's happiest occasions. Along the way, you'll learn how to wrap up a cake with a modeling chocolate wrap, ribbons, and bow (see the Pretty as a Package Cake on page 128), create a playful cake topper out of wired modeling chocolate balls for a burst of pure sugary joy (see the Two-Tiered Whimsy Cake on page 143), and craft glittering edible snowflakes that are just the thing to make everyone dream of a white—and 100 percent gluten-free—Christmas (see the White Christmas Bûche de Noël on page 148). Chapter 6 is chock-full of all the frostings, fillings, and glazes I turn to over and over again.

Want to give your gluten-free cakes the royal treatment? Just turn to "Tips, Tricks & Decorating Techniques" on page 169 and learn dozens of methods for crowning your cakes (and cupcakes) in style. With a little practice, you can pipe swirls, spikes, or mounds of buttercream; ornament your cakes with decorative borders; cover them with ruffled ribbons; sprinkle them with modeling chocolate confetti; or create a mirror-smooth finish that looks as if it were created by a professional pastry chef. You'll find loads of cake-decorating inspiration—and the know-how to execute it.

With all these recipes and tips, it's then up to you and your imagination to create your own beautifully decorated gluten-free cakes—because the best cake will always be the one you get to eat next!

1

BREAKFAST, SNACK & COFFEE
cakes

These unfussy recipes for simple everyday cakes are as close as it gets to no-fail, the perfect choice for new bakers—including pint-size aspirants who are excited to get in the kitchen and bake. While my family didn't have any serious baking enthusiasts, I developed a passion for baking from a very young age, and took to the kitchen to learn how to do it myself, beginning with the recipes I was least likely to mess up: coffee cakes.

So with a tip of my chef's hat to anyone who wants to roll up their sleeves and bake some cakes, I open this book with my gluten-free interpretations of uncomplicated, old-fashioned favorites that can be made in a single Bundt, tube, loaf, round, or rectangular pan. You'll find familiar classics to enjoy for breakfast, snacks, or anytime, but I've included lots of irresistible new recipes, too. Try a slice of my Honey-Lavender Tea Cake (page 17), Fruitcake with Citrus-Ginger Syrup (batter pictured opposite), or Lemon Blueberry Bundt with Glistening Lemon Glaze (page 16). These are cakes you can throw together on the spur of the moment, whenever the mood strikes.

I never had the opportunity to bake with my nana, but I did, on many occasions, devour her amazing banana cake, the inspiration for this gluten-free recipe. It's supermoist, with a crumb that's tender but not too delicate. I added raw cacao powder, which intensifies the banana flavor.

Nana Banana Snack Cake

ALMOND CRUMB TOPPING

½ cup lightly packed dark brown sugar

¼ cup chopped almonds (natural or blanched)

¼ cup almond meal (store-bought or homemade, page 197)

¼ cup melted and cooled virgin coconut oil (see page 193)

2 teaspoons ground cinnamon

BANANA CAKE

1¾ cups lightly packed dark brown sugar

1½ cups almond meal (store-bought or homemade, page 197)

1½ cups Gluten-Free Whole Grain Flour Blend (page 191)

¼ cup organic cacao powder (see page 195)

2 teaspoons baking powder

2 teaspoons ground cinnamon

1 teaspoon baking soda

1 teaspoon xanthan gum

½ teaspoon fine sea salt

4 eggs or Flax Egg Replacer (page 194), at room temperature

½ cup melted and cooled virgin coconut oil

3 ripe bananas, mashed

2 teaspoons pure vanilla extract

Preheat the oven to 350°F. Lightly oil a 9 by 13-inch cake pan with nonstick cooking spray or coconut oil.

To make the crumb topping: In a medium bowl, combine the brown sugar, almonds, almond meal, oil, and cinnamon, mixing with your fingertips or a whisk until well combined.

To make the cake: In a medium bowl, whisk together the brown sugar, almond meal, flour blend, cacao powder, baking powder, cinnamon, baking soda, xanthan gum, and salt. Set aside.

In the bowl of a stand mixer with the paddle attachment, combine the eggs, oil, bananas, and vanilla. Beat on medium-low for 1 minute, until well combined and fairly smooth. Add the flour mixture to the banana mixture and beat on medium-low for 1 minute more, until the batter is smooth.

Pour the batter into the prepared pan, filling the pan about half full. Spread the crumb topping over the batter, covering the cake almost completely. Bake in the center of the oven for about 35 minutes, until the edges are browned and the center of the cake tests clean with a toothpick. Transfer the cake to a wire rack to cool at least 15 minutes; slice and serve the cake directly from the pan while still warm or at room temperature.

To store, tightly wrap the pan in plastic wrap, or transfer any leftover slices to a large resealable plastic bag or airtight container. Keep at room temperature for 1 to 2 days or in the refrigerator for 5 to 7 days. Or you can freeze it, tightly wrapped in a double layer of plastic wrap, up to 2 months; thaw at room temperature before removing the plastic and serving.

My version of this classic sponge cake is tender, is light as air, and, true to its name, tastes heavenly. Some angel food cake recipes suggest beating the whites to stiff peaks, but I call for soft peaks instead; this allows for more expansion during baking, resulting in a lighter cake. (For more pointers on how to achieve proper volume, see the tips below.) A fresh berry garnish is all that's needed to complete this divine dessert. And it's naturally low in fat—so feel free to indulge.

MAKES ONE 10-INCH-DIAMETER TUBE CAKE (14 TO 16 SERVINGS)

Angel Food Cake with Fresh Berries

¾ cup plus 6 tablespoons organic cane sugar

¾ cup Gluten-Free Whole Grain Flour Blend (page 191)

¼ cup cornstarch

1½ cups egg whites (about 12 large whites), at room temperature

1½ teaspoons cream of tartar

½ teaspoon fine sea salt

1 teaspoon pure vanilla extract

2 cups fresh berries (your choice)

Preheat the oven to 350°F.

In a medium bowl, combine ¾ cup of the sugar, the flour blend, and the cornstarch. Sift the mixture twice to thoroughly combine and aerate. In the bowl of a stand mixer with the whisk attachment, beat together the egg whites, cream of tartar, salt, and vanilla on medium speed until soft peaks form. Gradually beat in the remaining 6 tablespoons sugar, about 2 tablespoons at a time. Remove the bowl from the mixer and, holding the whisk attachment in your hand, blend in the flour mixture in three batches until just combined.

Gently pour the batter into an ungreased 10-inch-diameter tube pan. Use a butter knife to cut through the batter to remove air pockets, and then gently smooth the top with the back of a large spoon. Bake on the lowest oven rack for 45 minutes, until the top is golden brown and dry. Immediately invert the pan and set it on the tube-pan feet (the cake will cling to the sides of the pan); cool completely, about 45 minutes.

When the cake has cooled, run a knife around the edge and center of the pan and remove the cake from the pan, referring to page 172 for guidance, if necessary. When ready to serve, top slices or the entire cake with the fresh berries.

Store in an airtight container or large resealable plastic bag up to 2 days or refrigerate up to 5 days. Or you can freeze it, tightly wrapped in a double layer of plastic wrap, up to 2 months; thaw at room temperature before removing the plastic and serving.

TIPS

To achieve proper volume, it's super-important to use a clean, grease-free bowl and whisk when beating the egg whites (and there must be absolutely no yolk in the whites). Do not grease the tube pan before adding the batter. If the egg foam comes into contact with any grease, it will immediately begin to deflate. Use only metal utensils for mixing and transferring the batter to the pan; plastic and silicone can cause the batter to deflate.

3 cups Gluten-Free Whole Grain
Flour Blend (page 191)

2 teaspoons baking powder

2 teaspoons xanthan gum

½ teaspoon fine sea salt

1 cup (2 sticks) unsalted butter
or Earth Balance Vegan Buttery
Sticks, at room temperature

1¼ cups organic cane sugar

¾ cup lightly packed dark brown
sugar

2 eggs or Flax Egg Replacer
(page 194), at room temperature

1 cup buttermilk or dairy-free
buttermilk (page 194), at room
temperature

1 tablespoon pure vanilla extract

2 cups sliced fresh organic
peaches or thawed frozen
peaches (no sugar added)

Sweetie Peach, the nickname my dad and I called each other, is the inspiration for this cake. I'm partial to peaches, but you can pair this cake with blackberries, raspberries, or any fresh or frozen fruit you like. If you use frozen fruit, just be sure to thaw it and select fruit with no added sugar—this cake is already plenty sweet without it.

Buttermilk Bundt Cake
with Peaches

Preheat the oven to 350°F. Lightly oil a 10-inch-diameter Bundt pan with nonstick cooking spray or coconut oil.

In a medium bowl, whisk together the flour blend, baking powder, xanthan gum, and salt. Set aside.

In the bowl of a stand mixer with the paddle attachment, beat the butter on medium speed until light and fluffy, about 1 minute. Scrape down the bowl with a rubber spatula and beat again for 15 seconds. Add both of the sugars and continue beating on medium until light and fluffy, 1 minute more. Scrape down the bowl and beat for 15 seconds more. Add the eggs, one at a time, beating for 20 seconds after each addition. Scrape down the bowl and mix again for 10 seconds or until well combined. Add the buttermilk to the batter and mix on low for 30 seconds, and then on medium for 30 seconds more. (The buttermilk will not be fully incorporated at this point.) Add the vanilla and mix for 15 seconds or until the batter is well combined.

With the mixer running on low speed, add the flour mixture to the buttermilk mixture, 1 cup at a time. Scrape down the bowl after the second and third additions. When all the flour has been added to the batter, increase the speed to medium and beat for 30 seconds until thoroughly incorporated.

Scrape the batter into the prepared pan. Bake in the center of the oven for 35 to 45 minutes, until the cake is light golden brown and set to the touch. Allow the cake to cool on a wire rack for 15 minutes before removing the cake from the pan to cool completely, referring to page 172 for guidance, if necessary. Slice the cake and serve with the peach slices.

Store in an airtight container or large resealable plastic bag at room temperature for 1 to 2 days or in the refrigerator for 5 to 7 days. Or you can freeze it, tightly wrapped in a double layer of plastic wrap, up to 2 months; thaw at room temperature before removing the plastic and serving.

This luscious riff on the traditional lemon–poppy seed coffee cake substitutes the tangy-sweet flavor of clementines in both the cake and the glaze. These tiny, red-orange citrus fruits are often available from April to November, but you can also use navel oranges. The glaze recipe makes enough icing to drip down the sides of the cake, but you can also pour extra over slices.

Poppy Seed Bundt Cake
with Clementine Glaze

POPPY SEED BUNDT CAKE

3 cups Gluten-Free Whole Grain Flour Blend (page 191)

¼ cup poppy seeds

2 teaspoons baking powder

1 teaspoon baking soda

1 teaspoon xanthan gum

½ teaspoon fine sea salt

1 cup (2 sticks) unsalted butter or Earth Balance Vegan Buttery Sticks, at room temperature

1½ cups organic cane sugar

4 eggs or Flax Egg Replacer (page 194), at room temperature

1 tablespoon freshly squeezed clementine juice

2 teaspoons clementine zest

1¼ cups buttermilk or nondairy buttermilk (see page 194)

Juice of 1 lemon

CLEMENTINE GLAZE

¼ cup freshly squeezed clementine juice (from about 3 clementines)

1½ to 2 cups confectioners' sugar (to make your own, see page 192)

Preheat the oven to 350°F. Lightly oil a 10-inch-diameter Bundt pan with nonstick cooking spray or coconut oil.

To make the cake: In a medium bowl, whisk together the flour blend, poppy seeds, baking powder, baking soda, xanthan gum, and salt. Set aside.

In the bowl of a stand mixer with the paddle attachment, beat the butter and sugar on medium speed for 2 minutes or until light and fluffy. Scrape down the bowl with a rubber spatula. While beating on low, slowly add the eggs. Then, increase the speed to medium and beat for 30 seconds. Add the clementine juice and zest and beat for 15 seconds on medium or until well combined. Scrape down the bowl.

Add one-fourth of the flour mixture to the egg mixture and beat on low until almost fully incorporated. Then, add one-third of the buttermilk and beat on low until almost fully incorporated. Repeat with the remaining flour and milk mixtures, starting and ending with the flour. When all the ingredients have been added, scrape down the bowl and beat on medium for 15 seconds.

Pour the batter into the prepared cake pan. Bake in the center of the oven for 45 to 50 minutes, until the top is golden brown and a toothpick inserted into the cake tests clean. Transfer the cake to a wire rack to cool for 10 minutes, and then invert the cake onto the rack to cool completely.

Meanwhile, make the glaze: In a small bowl, whisk the juice and 1½ cups confectioners' sugar until smooth. If the glaze looks thin, whisk in up to ½ cup more sugar.

When the cake is cool, place a parchment-lined baking sheet under the rack and pour the glaze over the cake. Allow the glaze to set up for 30 minutes before serving.

Store in an airtight container at room temperature for 1 to 2 days or in the refrigerator for 5 to 7 days. Or you can freeze it, tightly wrapped in a double layer of plastic wrap, up to 2 months; thaw at room temperature before removing the plastic and serving.

This beautiful Bundt was the first cake I hoped to make deliciously gluten free. I began by layering in the lemon flavor, using fresh juice and zest in both the batter and the glaze. Don't even think about using bottled juice here: the fresh flavor, aroma, and oils of fresh lemon are crucial to the success of this cake.

LEMONY BLUEBERRY BUNDT

3 cups Gluten-Free Whole Grain Flour Blend (page 191)

2 teaspoons baking powder

2 teaspoons xanthan gum

½ teaspoon fine sea salt

1 cup milk or unsweetened coconut milk (from a carton), at room temperature

1 tablespoon freshly squeezed lemon juice

1 tablespoon organic lemon zest

1 cup (2 sticks) unsalted butter or Earth Balance Vegan Buttery Sticks, at room temperature

2 cups organic cane sugar

2 eggs or Flax Egg Replacer (page 194), at room temperature

1 cup frozen organic blueberries

GLISTENING LEMON GLAZE

¼ cup freshly squeezed lemon juice

1 tablespoon finely chopped organic lemon zest

4 to 6 tablespoons confectioners' sugar (to make your own, see page 192)

Lemon Blueberry Bundt
with Glistening Lemon Glaze

Preheat the oven to 350°F. Lightly oil a 10-inch-diameter Bundt pan with nonstick cooking spray or coconut oil.

To make the cake: In a medium bowl, whisk together the flour blend, baking powder, xanthan gum, and salt. In a small bowl, mix the milk with the lemon juice and zest. Set both bowls aside.

Place the butter in the bowl of a stand mixer with the paddle attachment and beat on medium speed until light and fluffy, about 1 minute. Scrape down the bowl and beat again for 15 seconds. Add the sugar and continue beating until light and fluffy, 1 minute. Scrape down the bowl and beat for 15 seconds. Add the eggs, one at a time, beating for 20 seconds and scraping down the bowl after each addition. Add the milk mixture to the batter and mix on low for 30 seconds, and then on medium for 30 seconds. The batter will look separated at this point.

With the mixer running on low speed, add the flour mixture to the butter mixture, about 1 cup at a time. Scrape down the bowl after the second and third additions. When all the flour has been added, mix on medium speed for 30 seconds. Remove the bowl from the mixer and fold in the blueberries using a rubber spatula.

Scrape the batter into the prepared pan. Bake for 40 to 50 minutes, until the cake is light golden brown and set to the touch. (Don't use a toothpick test: this cake is very moist, and the blueberries may make the toothpick appear wet when the cake is actually done.) Transfer the cake in its pan to a wire rack to cool for 15 minutes.

Meanwhile, make the glaze: In a small bowl, whisk together the lemon juice, lemon zest, and confectioners' sugar. Use the smaller amount of sugar for a thinner glaze, and the larger amount if you want it thicker.

When the cake is cool to the touch, remove the cake from the pan to cool on a wire rack set over a parchment-lined baking sheet, referring to page 172 for guidance if necessary. When completely cool, pour the glaze over the top of the cake.

Store in an airtight container at room temperature for 1 to 2 days or in the refrigerator for 5 to 7 days. Or you can freeze it, tightly wrapped in a double layer of plastic wrap, up to 2 months; thaw at room temperature before removing the plastic and serving.

This lovely cake makes any occasion feel special. Pour a cup of tea, plate a slice, and you'll see what I mean. Dried lavender will make your glaze a beautiful pale blue. Fresh buds won't yield as intense a color and can be tricky to find (I mail-order mine), but the flavor will be more robust. See page 206 for a list of organic lavender and lavender extract purveyors.

Honey-Lavender Tea Cake

Preheat the oven to 350°F. Lightly grease a 10-inch-diameter Bundt pan with nonstick cooking spray or coconut oil.

To make the cake: In a medium bowl, whisk together the flour blend, baking powder, xanthan gum, and salt. In a small bowl, mix the milk and lavender extract. Set both bowls aside.

In the bowl of a stand mixer with the paddle attachment, beat the butter on medium speed until light and fluffy, about 1 minute. Scrape down the bowl and beat for 15 seconds. Add the sugar and continue beating on medium until the mixture is light and fluffy, 1 minute more. Scrape down the bowl and beat for 15 seconds. Add the eggs, one at a time, and beat on medium for 20 seconds, scraping down the bowl after each addition. Add the milk mixture to the batter and mix on low for 30 seconds, and then on medium for 30 seconds. The batter will look separated at this point.

With the mixer on low speed, add the flour mixture to the butter mixture, 1 cup at a time. Scrape down the bowl after the second and third additions. When all the flour has been added to the batter, mix on medium for 30 seconds until well combined.

Scrape the batter into the prepared pan. Bake in the center of the oven for about 40 minutes, until the cake is light golden brown. Transfer the pan to a wire rack to cool.

Meanwhile, make the glaze: In a small saucepan, combine the honey, lemon juice, and lavender and bring to a simmer, stirring to dissolve the honey. Continue simmering over medium heat until the mixture thickens, about 5 minutes, stirring often. Remove from the heat and set aside.

When the cake is cool to the touch, remove the cake from the pan to cool on a wire rack set over a parchment-lined baking sheet, referring to page 172 for guidance, if necessary. When completely cool, pour the glaze over the top of the cake. Sprinkle fresh lavender buds over the cake before the glaze sets.

Store in an airtight container at room temperature for 1 to 2 days or refrigerate for 5 to 7 days. If you want to freeze the cake, skip the lavender buds. Tightly wrap in a double layer of plastic wrap and freeze up to 2 months; thaw at room temperature before serving.

MAKES ONE 10-INCH-DIAMETER
BUNDT CAKE (12 TO 14 SERVINGS)

LAVENDER TEA CAKE

3 cups Gluten-Free Whole Grain Flour Blend (page 191)

2 teaspoons baking powder

2 teaspoons xanthan gum

½ teaspoon fine sea salt

1 cup milk or unsweetened coconut milk (from a carton), at room temperature

1 teaspoon pure lavender extract

1 cup (2 sticks) unsalted butter or Earth Balance Vegan Buttery Sticks, at room temperature

2 cups organic cane sugar

2 eggs or Flax Egg Replacer (page 194), at room temperature

HONEY-LAVENDER GLAZE

¼ cup raw honey or light agave nectar

1 tablespoon freshly squeezed lemon juice

2 teaspoons dried lavender or fresh lavender buds

Fresh lavender buds, for garnish (optional)

ESPRESSO STREUSEL

½ cup organic cane sugar

2 tablespoons unsalted butter
or Earth Balance Vegan Buttery
Sticks, at room temperature

½ teaspoon ground cinnamon

½ teaspoon instant espresso
powder

¼ cup dark chocolate chips

½ cup finely chopped walnuts

MOCHA COFFEE CAKE

2 cups Gluten-Free Whole Grain
Flour Blend (page 191)

1 teaspoon xanthan gum

1 teaspoon baking powder

1 teaspoon baking soda

1 teaspoon ground cinnamon

1 cup Greek yogurt or dairy-free
yogurt (see page 194)

½ cup mashed ripe banana

½ cup (1 stick) unsalted butter
or Earth Balance Vegan Buttery
Stick, at room temperature

¾ cup organic cane sugar

3 eggs or Flax Egg Replacer
(page 194), at room temperature

1 teaspoon pure vanilla extract

1 tablespoon instant espresso
powder

1 teaspoon hot water

¾ cup dark chocolate chips

Espresso Cinnamon Glaze
(page 164)

Had a tough week at work? Are the kids making you a little crazy? Here's your reward: my favorite coffee cake with a jolt of espresso added to the batter, the streusel, *and* the glaze. Talk about layering flavors—a slice of this will knock your socks off. Oh, yeah, and there's dark chocolate, too. I know, you can thank me later. Be sure to use instant espresso powder (see page 196), not ground espresso beans.

Mocha Coffee Cake

Preheat the oven to 350°F. Lightly grease a 9-inch-diameter cake pan with nonstick cooking spray or coconut oil.

To make the streusel: In a small bowl, using a fork, mix together the sugar, butter, cinnamon, and espresso powder until well combined. (Don't use your fingers to mix the streusel because their heat will make the butter too soft.) Add the chocolate chips and nuts and toss to combine. Set aside.

To make the cake: In a medium bowl, whisk together the flour blend, xanthan gum, baking powder, baking soda, and cinnamon. In a small bowl, mix the yogurt and mashed banana. Set both bowls aside.

In the bowl of a stand mixer with the paddle attachment, beat the butter with the sugar on medium speed until creamy. Scrape down the bowl with a rubber spatula. Add the eggs one at a time, beating on medium for 15 seconds after each addition. Mix in the vanilla and scrape down the bowl. Combine the espresso powder and hot water and mix until a paste is formed. Add the espresso paste to the batter and mix for 15 seconds or until well combined.

Add half the flour mixture to the butter mixture, mixing on medium-low for 15 seconds. Add half the banana mixture, mixing on medium-low for 15 seconds. Repeat with the remaining flour and banana mixtures. Scrape down the bowl. Fold in the chocolate chips, using a rubber spatula to evenly distribute the chips.

Scrape the batter into the prepared pan, filling the pan about halfway full. Spread the streusel topping over the batter. Bake in the center of the oven for 35 to 45 minutes, until the topping is light golden and a toothpick inserted tests clean. Transfer the pan to a wire rack to cool completely.

Meanwhile, make the glaze. When the cake is cool to the touch, transfer the cake from the pan to a wire rack set over a parchment-lined baking sheet; see page 172 for guidance. Pour the glaze over the top of the cake while still warm.

Store in an airtight container or large resealable plastic bag at room temperature for 1 to 2 days or in the refrigerator for 5 to 7 days. Or you can freeze it, tightly wrapped in a double layer of plastic wrap, up to 2 months; thaw at room temperature before removing the plastic and serving.

Cinnamon and almond streusel is the name of the game here—it makes this coffee cake so decadently apple-pie-like. You'll notice that I don't use any flour in my streusel. This allows the butter and sugar mixture to melt into the cake a little, creating a sugary-nutty crust rather than a heavy crumb that just sits on top of the cake.

Apple-Cinnamon Coffee Cake
with Almond Streusel

ALMOND STREUSEL

2 tablespoons unsalted butter or Earth Balance Vegan Buttery Stick, at room temperature

½ cup organic cane sugar

1 teaspoon ground cinnamon

½ cup finely chopped natural almonds (brown skins on)

APPLE-CINNAMON COFFEE CAKE

2 cups Gluten-Free Whole Grain Flour Blend (page 191)

1 teaspoon xanthan gum

1 teaspoon baking powder

1 teaspoon baking soda

1 teaspoon ground cinnamon

1 cup Greek yogurt or dairy-free yogurt (see page 194)

½ cup natural applesauce (no sugar added)

½ cup (1 stick) unsalted butter or Earth Balance Vegan Buttery Stick, at room temperature

¾ cup organic cane sugar

3 eggs or Flax Egg Replacer (page 194), at room temperature

1 teaspoon pure vanilla extract

1 cup peeled and chopped Granny Smith apples

Preheat the oven to 350°F. Lightly oil a 9-inch-diameter cake pan with nonstick cooking spray or coconut oil.

To make the streusel: In a small bowl, using a fork, mix together the butter, sugar, and cinnamon until well combined. (Don't use your fingers to mix the streusel because their heat will make the butter too soft.) Add the almonds and toss to combine. Set aside.

To make the cake: In a medium bowl, whisk together the flour blend, xanthan gum, baking powder, baking soda, and cinnamon. In a small bowl, mix the yogurt with the applesauce. Set both bowls aside.

In the bowl of a stand mixer with the paddle attachment, beat the butter and sugar on medium speed just until creamy. Scrape down the bowl with a rubber spatula. Add the eggs, one at a time, beating on medium for 15 seconds after each addition to thoroughly combine. Mix in the vanilla, and then scrape down the bowl.

Add half the flour mixture to the butter mixture and mix on medium-low for 15 seconds. Add half the yogurt mixture and mix on medium-low for 15 seconds. Repeat with the remaining flour and yogurt mixtures. Scrape down the bowl. Fold in the apples, using a rubber spatula to evenly distribute them.

Scrape the batter into the prepared pan, filling the pan about half full. Spread the streusel topping over the batter, covering the cake almost completely. Bake in the center of the oven for 35 to 45 minutes, until a toothpick inserted into the center tests clean. Allow the cake to cool for 15 minutes before removing the cake from the pan, referring to page 172 for guidance, if necessary. Flip the cake, streusel-side up, and let cool completely.

Store in an airtight container or large resealable plastic bag at room temperature for 1 to 2 days or in the refrigerator for 5 to 7 days. Or you can freeze it, tightly wrapped at room temperature before removing the plastic and serving.

Bursting with warm autumnal flavors, this cake will definitely be a welcome addition to your Thanksgiving spread, but I predict you won't want to wait until November to enjoy a slice. This light cake has just a subtle hint of pumpkin flavor—the emphasis here is on the spices. A sweet cinnamon-and-vanilla glaze makes it guestworthy.

Pumpkin Spice Cake
with Creamy Cinnamon Glaze

Preheat the oven to 350°F. Lightly oil a 9-inch-diameter cake pan with nonstick cooking spray or coconut oil.

To make the cake: In a medium bowl, whisk together the flour blend, cinnamon, xanthan gum, baking powder, baking soda, and pumpkin pie spice. In a small bowl, mix the yogurt and pumpkin puree. Set both bowls aside.

In the bowl of a stand mixer with the paddle attachment, beat the butter and sugar on medium speed until just creamed. (You don't need to beat until light and fluffy.) Scrape down the bowl with a rubber spatula before continuing. Add the eggs, one at a time, beating for 15 seconds after each addition. Mix in the vanilla, and then scrape down the bowl again.

Add half the flour mixture to the butter mixture, mixing on medium-low for 15 seconds. Add half the pumpkin mixture, mixing on medium-low for 15 seconds. Repeat with the remaining flour and pumpkin mixtures until well combined. Scrape down the bowl.

Scrape the batter into the prepared pan, filling the pan about halfway. Bake in the center of the oven for 35 to 40 minutes, until the top is golden brown and a toothpick inserted into the center tests clean.

Meanwhile, make the glaze: In a small bowl, whisk together the coconut milk, cinnamon, vanilla, and confectioners' sugar until smooth.

When the cake is done, transfer the pan to a wire rack to cool for 15 minutes before removing the cake from the pan, referring to page 172 for guidance, if necessary. Place a parchment-lined baking sheet under the rack and let the cake cool completely before pouring the glaze over the top.

Store in an airtight container or large resealable plastic bag at room temperature for 1 to 2 days or in the refrigerator for 5 to 7 days. Or you can freeze it, tightly wrapped in a double layer of plastic wrap, up to 2 months; thaw at room temperature before removing the plastic and serving.

PUMPKIN SPICE CAKE

2 cups Gluten-Free Whole Grain Flour Blend (page 191)

2 teaspoons ground cinnamon

1 teaspoon xanthan gum

1 teaspoon baking powder

1 teaspoon baking soda

1 teaspoon pumpkin pie spice

1 cup Greek yogurt or dairy-free yogurt (see page 194)

¾ cup canned pumpkin puree (not pumpkin-pie filling)

½ cup butter (1 stick) or Earth Balance Vegan Buttery Stick, at room temperature

¾ cup organic cane sugar

3 eggs or Flax Egg Replacer (page 194), at room temperature

1 teaspoon pure vanilla extract

CREAMY CINNAMON GLAZE

¼ cup canned unsweetened coconut milk (shake can before opening)

½ teaspoon ground cinnamon

½ teaspoon pure vanilla extract

1 tablespoon confectioners' sugar (to make your own, see page 192)

Polenta Breakfast Cake (page 24)

POLENTA CAKE

1½ cups Gluten-Free Whole
Grain Flour Blend (page 191)

1 cup almond meal (see page 197)

1 cup finely ground polenta
or cornmeal

½ teaspoon xanthan gum

1 cup finely chopped natural
almonds (brown skins on)

1 cup (2 sticks) unsalted butter
or Earth Balance Vegan Buttery
Sticks, at room temperature

1 cup organic cane sugar

2 teaspoons organic orange zest

3 eggs or Flax Egg Replacer
(page 194), at room temperature

½ cup freshly squeezed orange
juice, at room temperature

2 teaspoons pure vanilla extract

12 whole natural almonds (brown
skins on), for garnish

HONEY-CITRUS SYRUP

Juice of 2 lemons

Juice of 2 oranges

2 tablespoons raw honey or
maple syrup

This cake (shown on page 22) has a texture that I can only describe as pleasantly toothsome. It's dense and nutty, which makes it particularly satisfying for breakfast or as an afternoon snack with a cup of tea. Don't skip the honey glaze—it comes together in a flash and elevates this already irresistible cake to extraordinary.

Polenta Breakfast Cake
with Honey-Citrus Syrup

Preheat the oven to 350°F. Lightly oil a 9-inch-diameter cake pan with nonstick cooking spray or coconut oil, and then line the bottom of the pan with parchment paper. (Don't be tempted to skip the parchment—this cake tends to stick to the bottom of the pan.)

To make the cake: In a medium bowl, whisk together the flour blend, almond meal, polenta, and xanthan gum. Stir in the chopped almonds.

In the bowl of a stand mixer fitted with the paddle attachment, beat the butter and sugar on medium speed until light and fluffy, about 2 minutes. Scrape down the bowl. Add the orange zest and beat until incorporated. Add the eggs, orange juice, and vanilla and mix on low to combine, then on medium for 30 seconds until incorporated. Remove the bowl from the mixer and fold in the flour mixture.

Scrape the batter into the prepared pan and smooth the top with the spatula. Arrange the whole almonds on top in a decorative fashion. I like to line the top edge of the cake (think of the almonds as the numbers on a clock face), and then place three to five almonds in the center to create a star shape. Bake in the center of the oven for 35 to 45 minutes, until a toothpick inserted into the center tests clean.

While the cake bakes, make the syrup: In a small saucepan, combine the lemon and orange juices with the honey and bring to a simmer over medium heat, stirring to dissolve the honey. Continue simmering, stirring often, until the mixture thickens and forms a thin syrup, about 5 minutes. Set aside to cool.

When the cake is done baking, transfer the pan to a wire rack. While the cake is still hot, prick the surface with a toothpick and pour the glaze over the top. Allow the cake to cool completely before removing it from the pan, or slice and serve directly from the pan while the cake is still warm.

To store, tightly wrap the pan in plastic wrap, or transfer any leftover slices to a large resealable plastic bag or airtight container. Keep at room temperature for 1 to 2 days or in the refrigerator for 5 to 7 days. Or you can freeze it up to 2 months; thaw at room temperature before removing the plastic and serving.

I've used fresh cherries in place of the classic maraschinos because they taste better and don't have any sugary syrups or dyes. If fresh cherries aren't in season, just skip them or add some halved pecans instead.

Pineapple Upside-Down Cake

Preheat the oven to 350°F.

To make the pineapple topping: Place the butter in a 9 by 13-inch cake pan and melt it in the oven. Remove the pan from the oven and sprinkle the brown sugar evenly over the melted butter; arrange the pineapple rings on top in a single layer. Place a cherry half inside each pineapple ring. Set aside.

To make the cake: In a medium bowl, whisk together the flour blend, baking powder, xanthan gum, and salt. In a small bowl, mix the milk and vanilla extract. Set both aside.

In the bowl of a stand mixer fitted with the paddle attachment, beat the butter on medium speed until light and fluffy, about 1 minute. Scrape down the bowl and beat again for 15 seconds. Add the sugar and continue beating on medium until light and fluffy, about 1 minute. Scrape down the bowl and beat for 15 seconds.

Crack the eggs into a small bowl and use a fork to lightly break up the yolks. Add the eggs to the butter mixture in two batches, beating on medium for 20 seconds after each addition. Scrape down the bowl and mix until well combined.

With the mixer running on low speed, add the flour mixture, 1 cup at a time. Scrape down the bowl after all the flour has been added, and then mix on medium for 15 seconds. Add the milk mixture to the batter and mix on low for 15 seconds and then on medium for 30 seconds to combine.

Pour the batter into the pan, evenly covering the pineapple. Bake for about 40 minutes, until the cake is light golden and a toothpick inserted into the center tests clean.

Transfer the pan to a wire rack and, while still hot, run a knife around the edge to loosen the cake. Place a serving platter or cutting board upside down over the top of the pan and carefully invert it. Leave the pan on the cake for about 10 minutes to allow the pineapple juices to run into the cake. Remove the pan and allow the cake to cool completely, or serve warm.

Store in a large resealable plastic bag or airtight container. Keep at room temperature for 1 to 2 days or in the refrigerator for 5 to 7 days. Or you can freeze it, tightly wrapped in a double layer of plastic wrap, up to 2 months; thaw at room temperature before removing the plastic and serving.

MAKES ONE 9 BY 13-INCH CAKE
(12 TO 16 SERVINGS)

PINEAPPLE TOPPING

½ cup (1 stick) unsalted butter or Earth Balance Vegan Buttery Stick

2 cups lightly packed dark brown sugar

2 (20-ounce) cans unsweetened pineapple slices in juice, drained, or 12 to 16 rings fresh, ripe pineapple

2 cups pitted and halved fresh cherries or pecan halves

VANILLA CAKE

2 cups plus 2 tablespoons Gluten-Free Whole Grain Flour Blend (page 191)

2 teaspoons baking powder

1 teaspoon xanthan gum

1 teaspoon fine sea salt

½ cup milk or unsweetened coconut milk (from a carton), at room temperature

1 tablespoon pure vanilla extract

1 cup (2 sticks) unsalted butter or Earth Balance Vegan Buttery Sticks, at room temperature

1 cup organic cane sugar

4 eggs or Flax Egg Replacer (page 194), at room temperature

FRUITCAKE

1 cup Gluten-Free Whole Grain
Flour Blend (page 191)

2 teaspoons baking powder

1 teaspoon peeled, finely grated
fresh ginger

½ teaspoon xanthan gum

2 teaspoons baking powder

½ teaspoon fine sea salt

½ teaspoon ground cinnamon

½ cup (1 stick) unsalted butter
or Earth Balance Vegan Buttery
Stick, at room temperature

½ cup organic cane sugar

¼ cup lightly packed dark brown
sugar

2 teaspoons pure vanilla extract

3 eggs or Flax Egg Replacer
(page 194), at room temperature

Zest of 1 lemon (reserve the
lemon to make the syrup)

Zest of 1 orange (reserve the
orange to make the syrup)

½ cup milk or unsweetened
coconut milk (from a carton)

1¼ cups chopped pecans

¾ cup dried apricots, chopped

½ cup dried blueberries

⅓ cup dried cranberries

These days, most of us don't have the time to nurse a fruitcake with booze for two weeks before Christmas is upon us. Instead, try these fast-track fruitcakes: they can be made in two hours flat, from preheating the oven to wrapping them up with a bow. The secret? Forgo the booze and give these moist, nut- and fruit-laden cakes a quick soak in a tart ginger-citrus syrup instead. The recipe calls for two recyclable foil pans (one mini, one medium), which yield tall, nicely proportioned loaves; give one as a gift and enjoy the other yourself. But if you prefer, you can bake this batter in a single 9 by 5-inch loaf pan; the recipe also doubles easily.

Fruitcake
with Citrus-Ginger Syrup

Preheat the oven to 325°F. Lightly oil one recyclable mini foil loaf pan and one 8 by 4-inch foil loaf pan with nonstick cooking spray or coconut oil.

To make the cake: In a medium bowl, whisk together the flour blend, baking powder, ginger, xanthan gum, salt, and cinnamon. Set aside.

In the bowl of a stand mixer fitted with the paddle attachment, beat the butter and both sugars on medium speed until light and fluffy. Scrape down the bowl with a rubber spatula. Add the vanilla and eggs and beat on medium for 30 seconds to fully incorporate. Add the flour mixture to the butter mixture and beat on low until well combined. Scrape down the bowl. Add the lemon and orange zests and beat on low until combined. While beating on low, add the milk, and then beat for 30 seconds on medium until combined. Scrape down the bowl and remove it from the mixer.

Using a rubber spatula or wooden spoon, fold the pecans, the dried fruits (see Tip, page 28), and the crystallized ginger into the batter until evenly distributed. Scrape the batter into the pans and firmly rap them once against the countertop to eliminate air bubbles. Smooth the tops with the back of a spoon and bake until the top is golden brown and a tester inserted into the center comes out clean, 45 minutes to 1 hour for the mini loaf and 1 hour to 1 hour 15 minutes for the larger loaf.

ingredients and method continued >>

⅓ cup golden raisins

⅓ cup dried cherries

¼ cup dried currants

¼ cup finely chopped
crystallized ginger

CITRUS-GINGER SYRUP

2 lemons (including zested lemon
from above)

2 or 3 oranges (including zested
orange from above)

2 tablespoons finely chopped
crystallized ginger

Meanwhile, make the syrup: Remove and reserve the zest from 1 lemon and 1 orange. Juice 2 lemons and 2 oranges into a liquid measuring cup; you should have ¾ cup to 1 cup juice total. If you need more juice, juice the third orange. In a heavy-bottomed saucepan, combine the juice, zest, and chopped ginger and bring to a boil over medium-high heat. Continue to boil, stirring occasionally, until the mixture thickens and is reduced to about ¼ cup syrup, 10 to 15 minutes. Remove from the heat and set aside.

When the cakes are done baking, transfer them to a wire rack, with a parchment-lined baking sheet underneath to catch any drips, and pour the syrup over the hot cakes. Allow the cakes to cool completely before removing them from the pans (see page 172 for guidance).

Store the cakes in airtight containers or large resealable plastic bags at room temperature for 2 to 4 days or in the refrigerator for 10 to 14 days. Or you can freeze them, each tightly wrapped in a double layer of plastic wrap, up to 2 months (or much longer, if you've wrapped them very securely); thaw at room temperature before removing the plastic and serving.

TIP

Feel free to personalize this fruitcake by using a different combination of nuts and fruits. Just keep the total quantities the same: 1¼ cups of nuts and 2¾ cups of assorted dried fruits.

The recipe is a tribute to Mrs. Bakke, a brilliant cook whose confident use of spices inspired the robust combination used in this moist gingerbread cake. The cinnamon, cardamom, ginger, and black pepper deliver heat and complex flavor, while the coconut oil, molasses, and brown sugar ensure that the cake is moist and sweet. The gingery citrus glaze soaks in and lends a subtle sheen.

Gingerbread Cake
with Fresh Ginger and Citrus Glaze

Preheat the oven to 350°F. Lightly grease a 9-inch-diameter pan with nonstick cooking spray or coconut oil.

To make the cake: In a medium bowl, whisk together the flour blend, xanthan gum, cinnamon, cardamom, ground ginger, salt, and pepper. In another large bowl, whisk together the oil, molasses, and brown sugar. Set both bowls aside.

Bring the water to a boil in a small saucepan, and then whisk the baking soda into the water. Add the baking soda mixture to the molasses mixture and whisk to incorporate. Whisk in the fresh ginger. Add the flour mixture to the molasses mixture, stirring to combine (no electric mixer required). Lightly beat the eggs in a cup to break up the yolks, and then stir them into the batter just until combined (no need to beat).

Pour the batter into the prepared pan. Bake in the center of the oven for about 45 minutes, until a toothpick inserted into the center tests clean.

Meanwhile, prepare the glaze: In a medium bowl, whisk together the confectioners' sugar, orange juice, lemon juice, orange zest, and lemon zest.

When the cake is done baking, transfer the pan to a wire rack to cool for about 15 minutes. Pour the glaze over the top of the cake while still warm. Allow the cake to cool completely before removing from the pan, referring to page 172 for guidance, if necessary, or slice and serve directly from the pan while the cake is still warm.

To store, tightly wrap the pan in plastic wrap, or transfer any leftover slices to a large resealable plastic bag or airtight container. Keep at room temperature for 1 to 2 days or in the refrigerator for 5 to 7 days. Or you can freeze it up to 2 months; thaw at room temperature before removing the plastic and serving.

MAKES ONE 9-INCH-DIAMETER CAKE
(10 TO 12 SERVINGS)

GINGERBREAD CAKE

2½ cups Gluten-Free Whole Grain Flour Blend (page 191)

1 teaspoon xanthan gum

1 teaspoon ground cinnamon

1 teaspoon ground cardamom

1 teaspoon ground ginger

½ teaspoon fine sea salt

½ teaspoon ground black pepper

¾ cup melted and cooled virgin coconut oil (see page 193)

¾ cup mild (not blackstrap) molasses

¾ cup packed dark brown sugar

¾ cup water

2 teaspoons baking soda

⅓ cup peeled, finely grated fresh ginger

2 eggs or Flax Egg Replacer (page 194), at room temperature

FRESH GINGER AND CITRUS GLAZE

½ cup confectioners' sugar (to make your own, see page 192)

1 tablespoon freshly squeezed orange juice

1 tablespoon freshly squeezed lemon juice

1 teaspoon organic orange zest

1 teaspoon organic lemon zest

MARBLED CAKE

3 cups Gluten-Free Whole Grain
Flour Blend (page 191)

2 teaspoons baking powder

1½ teaspoons xanthan gum

½ teaspoon fine sea salt

1 cup milk or unsweetened
coconut milk (from a carton),
at room temperature

2 teaspoons pure vanilla extract

¾ cup (1½ sticks) unsalted butter
or Earth Balance Vegan Buttery
Sticks, at room temperature

1½ cups plus 3 tablespoons
organic cane sugar

3 eggs or Flax Egg Replacer
(page 194), at room temperature

5 tablespoons natural
(nonalkalized) cocoa powder

3 tablespoons hot tap water

Glossy Chocolate Glaze
(page 164)

Chocolate and vanilla batter are swirled together to create a sweet, dense cake that's reminiscent of pound cake. A glossy chocolaty glaze is drizzled over the top to make these cakes even more irresistible. Because two loaves are twice as nice, I've used a pair of foil pans. They're smaller than most metal loaf pans, which gives you a taller loaf. This cake is sturdy enough for toasting, so it's extra-nice for snacking, but if you want to toast your slices, you'll have to sacrifice the glaze.

Chocolate and Vanilla Marbled Cakes

Preheat the oven to 350°F. Lightly oil two 8 by 4-inch recyclable foil loaf pans with nonstick cooking spray or coconut oil.

To make the cake: In a medium bowl, whisk together the flour blend, baking powder, xanthan gum, and salt. In a small bowl, mix together the milk and vanilla. Set both bowls aside.

In the bowl of a stand mixer with the paddle attachment, beat the butter and 1½ cups of the sugar on medium speed for 2 minutes or until light and fluffy. Scrape down the bowl with a rubber spatula. While beating on low, slowly add the eggs. When all the eggs have been added, increase the speed to medium and beat for 30 seconds more. Scrape down the bowl.

Add one-fourth of the flour mixture to the butter mixture and beat on low until almost fully incorporated. Add one-third of the milk mixture and beat on low until almost fully incorporated. Repeat with the remaining flour and milk mixtures, starting and ending with the flour. When all the ingredients have been added, scrape down the bowl and beat on medium for 15 seconds.

Transfer half the batter to a separate bowl. In a small bowl, combine the cocoa powder, the remaining 3 tablespoons sugar, and the hot water and stir or whisk to combine. Add the cocoa mixture to one bowl of the batter and stir to form a chocolate batter.

Drop large spoonfuls of both batters on the bottom of the prepared pans, alternating white and chocolate batter. Repeat with a second layer of batter, placing chocolate on top of white and white on top of chocolate to create a casual checkerboard effect. Using the handle of a wooden spoon, swirl the batter into a marble pattern. Tap the pans firmly on the countertop to settle the batter and remove air pockets.

Bake in the center of the oven for 50 to 55 minutes, until the cakes are set to the touch and a toothpick inserted into the center tests clean. The cakes will be lightly browned and the tops may crack slightly down the middle. (Don't worry—the glaze will mask any cracks.) Cool the cakes on a wire rack for about 10 minutes. When the cakes are cool to the touch, remove them from the pans to a rack set over a parchment-lined baking sheet (see page 172 for guidance, if necessary) and let cool.

While the cakes cool, make the glaze. Allow it to cool just until lukewarm, and then pour the glaze over the cakes, allowing it to drip over the edges. Serve immediately.

To store, allow the glaze to set up for at least 1 hour, and then lightly wrap the cakes separately with plastic wrap. The cakes will keep at room temperature for 1 to 2 days or in the refrigerator for 5 to 7 days. To freeze, do not glaze the cakes; wrap tightly in a double layer of plastic wrap and freeze up to 2 months; thaw at room temperature before removing the plastic and glazing the cakes.

CHOCOLATE SHEET CAKE

½ cup buttermilk or nondairy
buttermilk (see page 194)

1 cup (2 sticks) unsalted butter or
Earth Balance Buttery Sticks

6 tablespoons natural
(nonalkalized) cocoa powder

1 cup boiling water

2 cups Gluten-Free Whole Grain
Flour Blend (page 191)

1½ cups organic cane sugar

½ cup lightly packed dark brown
sugar

1 teaspoon baking soda

½ teaspoon fine sea salt

¼ teaspoon xanthan gum

2 eggs or Flax Egg Replacer
(page 194)

2 teaspoons pure vanilla extract

Chocolate Icing (page 164)

We Texans are known for going big, and this jumbo chocolaty sheet cake with a rich chocolate icing is no exception. It's also proof that you don't need a mixer or special pans to make an irresistible cake: just mix the batter with a whisk (brown sugar maximizes the moistness and flavor), bake, pour the icing on top, and serve right out of the pan. You don't even have to remember to pull the butter out of the fridge early because you'll be melting it. While most cakes need to come to room temperature for best flavor, this cake tastes equally good straight from the fridge, which facilitates instant snacking gratification all week long.

Texas Sheet Cake

Preheat the oven to 350°F. Spray a 13 by 18-inch jelly-roll pan with nonstick cooking spray, line the pan with parchment paper, and spray again.

To make the cake: If you are making a nondairy cake, prepare the nondairy buttermilk and set aside to allow the buttermilk flavor to develop. Melt the butter in a medium saucepan over medium heat. Add the cocoa powder to the melted butter and whisk until well combined. Bring the chocolate mixture to a simmer; reduce the heat to low and cook for 2 minutes, stirring occasionally. Add the boiling water and whisk to combine; continue cooking for 1 minute over low heat. Remove from the heat and allow to cool for 1 minute.

In a large bowl, whisk together the flour blend, cane sugar, brown sugar, baking soda, salt, and xanthan gum. Pour the hot chocolate mixture over the dry ingredients and combine using a large whisk. Add the buttermilk, eggs, and vanilla and whisk until well combined.

Pour the batter into the prepared pan and, using a rubber spatula, spread the batter to the edges of the pan and into the corners. Bake for 17 to 20 minutes, until the center of the cake feels firm to the touch and a toothpick inserted into the center tests clean. Transfer the cake in its pan to a wire rack to cool while you make the icing.

While the cake is still warm, pour the icing over the cake and, with a spatula or the back of a large spoon, spread the icing to the edges of the cake and into the corners. Cool the cake completely before cutting into squares to serve from the pan.

To store, wrap the pan tightly in plastic wrap; the cake will keep at room temperature for 1 to 2 days or in the refrigerator for 5 to 7 days. If you want to freeze the cake, do not ice it: wrap the pan tightly in a double layer of plastic wrap and freeze for up to 1 month. Thaw at room temperature before icing the cake.

2

LAYER
cakes

When most of us think about cake (hopefully often, with joy in our hearts!), we envision lots of soft, tender layers; an irresistibly sweet filling; and generous swirls of icing covering it all. You're bound to find gluten-free versions of many of your favorites here—classic chocolate, southern coconut, hummingbird, and German chocolate among them—each paired with a delectable filling and icing duo. But I've also included fresh flavor combinations, including Pink Velvet Strawberry Cake (page 52), Chocolate Peppermint Cake (page 64), and Caramel Cream Cake (page 60), that I hope will entice you into the kitchen.

You can build the flavor in a layer cake by repeating a signature flavor note in two or three of the elements. This is a trick I learned as a professional pastry chef, where the mantra was to keep the flavoring subtle (and natural!) and repeat it throughout the dessert's components. The resulting baked good has a more fully developed flavor profile and is far more palate-pleasing than if you heavily doused one component with a flavoring (or used artificial extracts). In the Pink Velvet Strawberry Cake, for example, I use fresh and frozen strawberries and jam in the filling, and then add a little strawberry puree to both the cake and the buttercream. Fresh strawberries are the optional garnish.

The secret to successful cake baking is planning ahead. All of these cakes have components that can be prepared in advance; in fact, they can all be baked up to a month ahead and kept in the freezer until you're ready to fill and ice it. Buttercreams and fruit purees can be frozen for a month or refrigerated for five days. Ganaches can be refrigerated for a week and curds for three days.

LEMON CURD

6 egg yolks (reserve the whites
to use in the cake)

¾ cup organic cane sugar

⅓ cup freshly squeezed lemon
juice

½ cup (1 stick) cold unsalted
butter or Earth Balance Vegan
Buttery Stick, cut into 16 cubes

LEMON CAKE

3 cups Gluten-Free All-Purpose
Flour Blend (page 191)

2 teaspoons baking powder

1½ teaspoons xanthan gum

½ teaspoon fine sea salt

1 cup milk or unsweetened
coconut milk (from a carton),
at room temperature

1 tablespoon freshly squeezed
lemon juice

2 teaspoons organic lemon zest

¾ cup (1½ sticks) unsalted butter
or Earth Balance Vegan Buttery
Sticks, at room temperature

1½ cups organic cane sugar

¾ cup egg whites (about 6 large
whites), at room temperature

Lemon Buttercream (page 159)

For lemon lovers everywhere, here's a lusciously lemony trifecta featuring lemon cake filled with lemon curd and slathered with a lickable lemon buttercream. It will make you pucker (in a good way). To festoon your cake with gorgeous buttercream roses, follow my instructions for covering a cake with piped star rosettes (see page 177). Any leftover lemon curd would be awesome layered with berries, as a filling for cakes, spread on toasted coffee cake, or eaten straight up with a spoon.

Triple Lemon Cake

To make the lemon curd: Prepare a double boiler by pouring 2 inches of water into a small saucepan and placing a shallow stainless steel bowl atop the pan so that the bottom does not touch the water (you want indirect heat; see Tip). Bring the water to a boil over high heat. In the top of the double boiler, whisk together the egg yolks, sugar, and lemon juice. Continue to whisk constantly until the sugar dissolves and the mixture thickens enough to coat the back of a spoon, 5 to 10 minutes. (Don't leave the egg-yolk mixture unattended over the double boiler; you must whisk constantly to avoid curdling or burning.) Remove from the heat and add the butter, two pieces at a time, whisking to melt. Allow each addition to melt almost completely before adding the next two pieces of butter. Pour the lemon curd into a clean bowl and cover with plastic wrap, pressing the plastic directly onto the surface of the curd to keep a skin from developing. Refrigerate until completely chilled and thickened, about 1 hour.

While the lemon curd chills, preheat the oven to 350°F. Lightly oil two 8-inch-diameter cake pans with nonstick cooking spray or coconut oil.

To make the cake: In a medium bowl, whisk together the flour blend, baking powder, xanthan gum, and salt. In a small bowl, mix the milk with the lemon juice and zest. Set both bowls aside.

In the bowl of a stand mixer with the paddle attachment, beat the butter and sugar on medium speed for 2 minutes or until light and fluffy. Scrape down the bowl with a rubber spatula. While beating on low speed, slowly add the egg whites. When all the whites have been added, increase the speed to medium and beat for 30 seconds. Scrape down the bowl.

Add one-fourth of the flour mixture to the butter mixture and beat on low until almost fully incorporated. Add one-third of the milk mixture and beat on low until almost fully incorporated. Repeat with the remaining flour and milk mixtures, starting and ending with the flour. When all the ingredients have been added, scrape down the bowl and beat on medium for 15 seconds.

Pour the batter into the prepared cake pans. Bake in the center of the oven for 30 to 35 minutes, until the tops are light golden and a toothpick inserted into the center tests clean. Cool the cakes on a wire rack for 10 minutes or until the pans are cool enough to handle safely, and then invert the cakes onto the rack to cool completely. (Allowing the cakes to cool in the pans will result in cakes with soggy bottoms.) Meanwhile, make the buttercream.

To assemble a two-layer cake, spread ¾ cup lemon curd between the layers, and then generously frost the top and sides of the cake with the buttercream, referring to the instructions on page 173 for guidance, if necessary. To create a four-layer cake, split each cake layer in half horizontally, following the procedure on page 173. Spread ½ cup lemon curd between each layer, and then generously frost the tops and sides with the buttercream.

The lemon curd can be refrigerated in an airtight container for only 3 days, so if you want to make the cake and frosting ahead, prepare them first. The filled and frosted cake can be stored in an airtight container at room temperature for 1 to 2 days or in the refrigerator for 5 to 7 days. To freeze, tightly wrap each unfrosted cake layer in a double layer of plastic wrap and freeze up to 1 month; thaw at room temperature before removing the plastic and filling and frosting the cake. The buttercream can be refrigerated in an airtight container for 5 days or frozen for 1 month.

TIP

When preparing the lemon curd, a stainless steel bowl is absolutely crucial. If you use an aluminum bowl, your curd will have a metallic taste.

VERY VANILLA CAKE

3 cups Gluten-Free All-Purpose
Flour Blend (page 191)

2 teaspoons baking powder

1½ teaspoons xanthan gum

½ teaspoon fine sea salt

1 cup milk or unsweetened
coconut milk (from a carton),
at room temperature

1 tablespoon pure vanilla extract

1 teaspoon vanilla bean paste
(optional; see page 196)

¾ cup (1½ sticks) unsalted butter
or Earth Balance Vegan Buttery
Sticks, at room temperature

1½ cups organic cane sugar

¾ cup egg whites (about 6 large
whites), at room temperature

Fudgy Frosting (page 166)

Here's everyone's favorite old-fashioned layer cake—vanilla cake with a rich
chocolate filling and icing—now blissfully gluten free. To punch up the intensity of
the flavors, I've suggested doubling up on the vanilla in the cake and using both
chocolate chips and cocoa in the frosting. If you like a sweeter frosting, substitute
milk chocolate chips. To finish the frosted cake with pretty swoops and swirls, see
the instructions on page 180. All you need is a spoon!

Very Vanilla Cake with Fudgy Frosting

Preheat the oven to 350°F. Lightly oil two 8-inch-diameter cake pans with nonstick
cooking spray or coconut oil.

To make the cake: In a medium bowl, whisk together the flour blend, baking
powder, xanthan gum, and salt. In a small bowl, mix the milk with the vanilla
extract and vanilla bean paste. Set both bowls aside.

In the bowl of a stand mixer with the paddle attachment, beat the butter and sugar
on medium speed for 2 minutes or until light and fluffy. Scrape down the bowl.
While beating on low, add the egg whites. When all the whites have been added,
increase the speed to medium and beat for 30 seconds. Scrape down the bowl.

Add one-fourth of the flour mixture to the butter mixture and beat on low until
almost fully incorporated. Add one-third of the milk mixture and beat on low
until almost fully incorporated. Repeat with the remaining flour and milk mixtures,
starting and ending with the flour. When all the ingredients have been added,
scrape down the bowl and beat on medium for 15 seconds.

Pour the batter into the prepared cake pans. Bake in the center of the oven for 30 to
35 minutes, until the tops are light golden and a toothpick inserted into the center
tests clean. Cool the cakes on a wire rack for 10 minutes, and then invert the cakes
onto the rack to cool completely. Meanwhile, make the frosting.

To assemble a two-layer cake, spread ¾ cup frosting between the layers and on the
top of the cake, and then generously frost the sides, referring to the instructions
on page 173 for guidance. To create a four-layer cake, split each cake layer in half
horizontally, following the procedure on page 173. Use ½ cup frosting between each
layer and on top of the cake, and then generously frost the sides.

You can store the frosted cake in an airtight container (or tented in plastic wrap) at
room temperature for 1 to 2 days or in the refrigerator for 5 to 7 days. Or the cake
layers can be frozen prior to filling and icing; wrap tightly in a double layer of plastic
wrap and freeze up to 2 months. Thaw at room temperature before removing the
plastic and filling and icing the cake. The frosting can be refrigerated in an airtight
container for 5 days or frozen for 1 month. Bring to room temperature and beat in
the bowl of a stand mixer to restore proper texture before using.

Swoops and swirls technique (page 180) shown on Very Vanilla Cake (page 40)

WHITE CAKE

3 cups Gluten-Free All-Purpose
Flour Blend (page 191)

2 teaspoons baking powder

1½ teaspoons xanthan gum

½ teaspoon fine sea salt

1 cup milk or unsweetened
coconut milk (from a carton),
at room temperature

2 teaspoons pure vanilla extract

¾ cup (1½ sticks) butter or Earth
Balance Vegan Buttery Sticks,
at room temperature

1½ cups organic cane sugar

¾ cup egg whites (about 6 large
whites), at room temperature

Very Vanilla Buttercream
(page 161)

1½ pounds ripe peaches

Juice of 1 lemon

This cake celebrates summer and all its lazy pleasures—and there's no better time to enjoy it than in May, June, and July, when peaches are at their peak. The peaches will release some of their juice into the cake layers, making this tender cake extra-moist and flavorful. You'll notice I don't add sugar to the peaches; the buttercream provides the perfect amount of sweetness to balance any acidity.

Peaches and Cream Cake

Preheat the oven to 350°F. Lightly oil two 8-inch-diameter cake pans with nonstick cooking spray or coconut oil.

To make the cake: In a medium bowl, whisk together the flour blend, baking powder, xanthan gum, and salt. In a small bowl, mix the milk with the vanilla. Set both bowls aside.

In the bowl of a stand mixer, beat the butter and sugar on medium speed for 2 minutes or until light and fluffy. Scrape down the bowl with a rubber spatula. While beating on low, slowly add the egg whites. When all the whites have been added, increase the speed to medium and beat for 30 seconds. Scrape down the bowl.

Add one-fourth of the flour mixture to the butter mixture and beat on low until almost fully incorporated. Add one-third of the milk mixture and beat on low until almost fully incorporated. Repeat with the remaining flour and milk mixtures, starting and ending with the flour. When all the ingredients have been added, scrape down the bowl and beat on medium for 15 seconds.

Pour the batter into the prepared cake pans. Bake in the center of the oven for 30 to 35 minutes, until the tops are light golden and a toothpick inserted tests clean. Transfer the cakes to a wire rack to cool for 10 minutes, and then invert onto the rack to cool. (Cooling in the pans will result in cakes with soggy bottoms.)

While the cakes bake and cool, make the buttercream. No more than 30 minutes before assembling, peel and slice the peaches, sprinkling them with the juice of 1 lemon to avoid discoloration. You should have about 4 cups.

To assemble a two-layer cake, scoop 1 cup of peach slices onto the bottom half of the cake, spreading them out to create an even layer. Top with the second cake layer, pressing down firmly. Frost the top and sides of the cake with the buttercream. To create a four-layer cake, split each cake layer in half horizontally. Scoop and evenly spread ½ cup of the peach slices between each layer, pressing down firmly on the cake before adding the next layer of peaches. Frost the top and sides of the cake with the buttercream. Garnish the top of the cake with the remaining peaches, or serve slices of the cake with peaches alongside.

The batter for this sweet southern classic, loved for its inclusion of pineapple, bananas, and pecans, goes together without much fuss. It's super-rich, so you can slice smaller servings, making it suitable for large gatherings. The use of white chocolate in the icing offers an unexpected twist that's sure to win rave reviews. Choose a high-quality white chocolate for the icing (for suggestions, see page 194). You only need a small quantity for this cake, so get the best you can afford—it will make a huge difference. Rosettes piped on the top of this cake make a stunning finish; for instructions, see page 177.

Hummingbird Cake
with White Chocolate Cream Cheese Icing

Preheat the oven to 350°F. Lightly oil two 8-inch-diameter cake pans with nonstick cooking spray or coconut oil.

To make the cake: In the bowl of a stand mixer with the paddle attachment, combine the flour blend, sugar, cinnamon, baking soda, xanthan gum, and salt. Mix on low speed to combine. Add the coconut oil, eggs, and vanilla and mix on low for 30 seconds, scraping down the bowl. The batter will be very thick and "sandy" at this point. Add the pineapple, orange juice, bananas, and pecans and mix on medium-low for 30 seconds to combine. Scrape down the bowl and mix again for 30 seconds to ensure that all the ingredients are thoroughly incorporated.

Pour the batter into the prepared cake pans. Bake in the center of the oven for 30 to 35 minutes, until the tops are light golden and a toothpick inserted into the center tests clean. Cool the cakes on a wire rack for 10 minutes or until the pans are cool enough to handle safely, and then invert the cakes onto the rack to cool completely. Allowing the cakes to cool completely in the pans will result in cakes with soggy bottoms. Meanwhile, make the icing.

To assemble a two-layer cake, spread ¾ cup icing between the layers and on the top of the cake, and then generously ice the sides, referring to the instructions on page 173 for guidance, if necessary. To create a four-layer cake, split each cake layer in half horizontally, following the procedure on page 173. Spread ½ cup icing between each layer and on top of the cake, then generously ice the sides.

You can store the finished cake in an airtight container at room temperature (or tented in plastic wrap) for 1 to 2 days or in the refrigerator for 5 to 7 days. Or you can freeze the un-iced layers, each tightly wrapped in a double layer of plastic wrap, up to 1 month; thaw at room temperature before removing the plastic and filling and icing the cake.

MAKES TWO 8-INCH-DIAMETER LAYERS (16 TO 20 SERVINGS)

HUMMINGBIRD CAKE

3 cups Gluten-Free All-Purpose Flour Blend (page 191)

1¾ cups organic cane sugar

2 teaspoons ground cinnamon

1 teaspoon baking soda

1 teaspoon xanthan gum

½ teaspoon fine sea salt

1¼ cups melted and cooled virgin coconut oil (see page 193)

3 eggs or Flax Egg Replacer (page 194), at room temperature

2 teaspoons pure vanilla extract

1 (8-ounce) can crushed pineapple, drained

⅓ cup freshly squeezed orange juice

3 ripe medium bananas, mashed

1 cup chopped pecans

White Chocolate Cream Cheese Icing (page 165)

Rosette decorating Technique (see page 177) shown on Hummingbird Cake (page 47)

The warm and toasty flavors of maple syrup, cinnamon, and walnuts make this a great cake for autumn. The quality of maple syrup you use is crucial because it provides the most prominent flavor in both the cake and the buttercream (see page 192 for help picking a maple syrup).

Maple Walnut Cake
with Cinnamon Maple Buttercream

MAPLE WALNUT CAKE

3 cups Gluten-Free All-Purpose Flour Blend (page 191)

2 teaspoons ground cinnamon

2 teaspoons baking powder

1½ teaspoons xanthan gum

½ teaspoon fine sea salt

1 cup milk or unsweetened coconut milk (from a carton), at room temperature

¼ cup maple syrup (see headnote)

2 teaspoons pure vanilla extract

¾ cup (1½ sticks) unsalted butter or Earth Balance Vegan Buttery Sticks, at room temperature

1½ cups organic cane sugar

¾ cup egg whites (about 6 large whites), at room temperature

1 cup chopped walnuts

Cinnamon Maple Buttercream (page 158)

½ cup chopped walnuts, for garnish

Preheat the oven to 350°F. Lightly oil two 8-inch-diameter cake pans with nonstick cooking spray or coconut oil.

To make the cake: In a medium bowl, whisk together the flour blend, cinnamon, baking powder, xanthan gum, and salt. In a small bowl, mix the milk, maple syrup, and vanilla. Set both bowls aside.

In the bowl of a stand mixer with the paddle attachment, beat the butter and sugar on medium speed for 2 minutes or until light and fluffy. Scrape down the bowl with a rubber spatula. While beating on low, slowly add the egg whites. Then, increase the speed to medium and beat for 30 seconds. Scrape down the bowl.

Add one-fourth of the flour mixture to the butter mixture and beat on low until almost fully incorporated. Then, add one-third of the milk mixture and beat on low until almost fully incorporated. Repeat with the remaining flour and milk mixtures, starting and ending with the flour. When all the ingredients have been added, scrape down the bowl and beat on medium for 15 seconds. Fold in the chopped walnuts until distributed.

Pour the batter into the prepared cake pans. Bake in the center of the oven for 30 to 35 minutes, until the tops are light golden and a toothpick inserted into the center tests clean. Cool the cakes on a wire rack for 10 minutes, and then invert the cakes onto the rack to cool completely. Meanwhile, make the buttercream.

To assemble a two-layer cake, spread ¾ cup buttercream between the layers and on the top of the cake, and then generously frost the sides (see page 173). To create a four-layer cake, split each cake layer in half horizontally (see page 173). Spread ½ cup buttercream between each layer and on top of the cake, and then frost the sides. Sprinkle the chopped walnuts around the top edge of the cake.

You can store the finished cake in an airtight container at room temperature for 1 to 2 days or in the refrigerator for 5 to 7 days. Or you can freeze the unfrosted cake layers, each wrapped in a double layer of plastic wrap, up to 1 month; thaw at room temperature before removing the plastic and filling and frosting the cake.

Real coconut is mild and nutty, aromatic and floral, and sublimely delicious, as this moist and flavorful old-fashioned layer cake attests. It's very important to use good-quality pure coconut extract and not the imitation stuff; it will make a huge difference in the flavor of this cake. Two brands that I like are Olive Nation and Flavorganics (see Sources on page 204).

Southern Coconut Cake

Preheat the oven to 350°F. Lightly oil two 8-inch-diameter cake pans with nonstick cooking spray or coconut oil.

To make the cake: In a medium bowl, whisk together the flour blend, baking powder, xanthan gum, and salt. In a small bowl, mix the milk and coconut extract. Set both bowls aside.

In the bowl of a stand mixer with the paddle attachment, beat the butter and sugar on medium speed for 2 minutes or until light and fluffy. Scrape down the bowl. While beating on low, slowly add the egg whites. When all the whites have been added, increase the speed to medium and beat for 30 seconds. Scrape down the bowl.

Add one-fourth of the flour mixture to the butter mixture and beat on low until almost fully incorporated. Then, add one-third of the milk mixture and beat on low until almost fully incorporated. Repeat with the remaining flour and milk mixtures, starting and ending with the flour. When all the ingredients have been added, scrape down the bowl and beat on medium for 15 seconds.

Pour the batter into the prepared cake pans. Bake in the center of the oven for 30 to 35 minutes, or until a toothpick inserted into the center tests clean. Transfer the cakes to a wire rack to cool for 10 minutes or until the pans are cool enough to handle safely, and then invert the cakes onto the rack to cool completely. Allowing the cakes to cool completely in the pans will result in cakes with soggy bottoms. Meanwhile, make the buttercream.

To assemble a two-layer cake, spread ¾ cup buttercream between the layers and on the top of the cake, and then generously frost the sides, referring to the instructions on page 173 for guidance, if necessary. To create a four-layer cake, split each cake layer in half horizontally, following the procedure on page 173. Spread ½ cup frosting between each layer and on top of the cake, and then generously frost the sides.

Press the toasted coconut onto the sides of the cakes or sprinkle the coconut over the top of the cake.

COCONUT CAKE

3 cups Gluten-Free All-Purpose Flour Blend (page 191)

2 teaspoons baking powder

1½ teaspoons xanthan gum

½ teaspoon fine sea salt

1 cup milk or unsweetened coconut milk (from a carton), at room temperature

1 teaspoon pure coconut extract

¾ cup (1½ sticks) unsalted butter or Earth Balance Vegan Buttery Sticks, at room temperature

1½ cups organic cane sugar

¾ cup egg whites (about 6 large whites), at room temperature

Coconut Buttercream (page 158)

½ to 1 cup unsweetened shredded or chipped coconut, toasted (see page 195)

STRAWBERRY PUREE

2 cups sliced fresh strawberries

1 cup frozen strawberries
(no sugar added)

½ cup frozen cherries (no sugar
added)

3 tablespoons organic cane sugar

1 tablespoon water

2 tablespoons any red fruit jam

**PINK VELVET STRAWBERRY
CAKE**

3 cups Gluten-Free All-Purpose
Flour Blend (page 191)

2 teaspoons baking powder

1½ teaspoons xanthan gum

½ teaspoon fine sea salt

½ cup milk or unsweetened
coconut milk (from a carton),
at room temperature

½ cup cooled Strawberry Puree
(above)

¾ cup (1½ sticks) unsalted butter
or Earth Balance Vegan Buttery
Sticks, at room temperature

1½ cups organic cane sugar

¾ cup egg whites (about 6 large
whites), at room temperature

Strawberry Buttercream
(page 161)

1½ cups fresh strawberries,
for garnish

A good strawberry cake is hard to find. A good strawberry cake recipe? Even harder. Natural strawberry flavor is quite subtle, so I like to use it within the cake batter itself, in the buttercream, and in the puree that's spread between the layers. The pink of the cake will be pale, not bright or garish. The buttercream will be a shade or two brighter, and the puree will be a vibrant pink-red, resulting in a lovely tricolor effect when the cake is sliced. Fresh strawberries on top are a pretty accent, but you can omit them if you prefer.

Pink Velvet Strawberry Cake
with Strawberry Buttercream

Make the strawberry puree first: You'll need some of it to flavor the cake batter and buttercream. In a medium saucepan over medium heat, combine the fresh and frozen strawberries, cherries, sugar, and water. Bring to a simmer and cook, stirring frequently with a wooden spoon until the sugar dissolves, and then only occasionally for about 15 minutes, or until the mixture thickens and the fruit has become soft enough to easily mash with the spoon.

Transfer the berry mixture to a shallow dish to cool for about 15 minutes, and then pour into a blender and blend until smooth. Add the jam and blend again. Refrigerate the blender pitcher until the puree has cooled, about 30 minutes. The puree can be made up to 2 days in advance and refrigerated in an airtight container.

Meanwhile, preheat the oven to 350°F. Lightly oil two 8-inch-diameter cake pans with nonstick cooking spray or coconut oil.

To make the cake: In a medium bowl, whisk together the flour blend, baking powder, xanthan gum, and salt. In a small bowl, mix the milk with the cooled strawberry puree. Set both bowls aside.

In the bowl of a stand mixer with the paddle attachment, beat the butter and sugar on medium speed for 2 minutes or until light and fluffy. Scrape down the bowl. While beating on low, slowly add the egg whites. When all the whites have been added, increase the speed to medium and beat for 30 seconds. Scrape down the bowl.

Add one-fourth of the flour mixture to the butter mixture and beat on low until almost fully incorporated. Add one-third of the milk mixture and beat on low until almost fully incorporated. Repeat with the remaining flour and milk mixtures, starting and ending with the flour. When all the ingredients have been added, scrape down the bowl and beat on medium for 15 seconds.

continued >>

Pink Velvet Strawberry Cake with Strawberry Buttercream, **continued >>**

Pour the batter into the prepared cake pans. Bake in the center of the oven for 30 to 35 minutes until the color darkens slightly and a toothpick inserted into the center tests clean. Cool the cakes on a wire rack for 10 minutes or until the pans are cool enough to handle safely, and then invert the cakes onto the rack to cool completely. Allowing the cakes to cool completely in the pans will result in cakes with soggy bottoms. Meanwhile, make the buttercream.

To assemble a two-layer cake, drizzle $\frac{1}{4}$ cup strawberry puree over one layer and spread it around with the back of a spoon to encourage some of it to soak into the cake. Smoothly spread $\frac{3}{4}$ cup buttercream on top of the puree, and then top with the second cake layer, pressing down firmly. Frost the top and sides of the cake with the buttercream, referring to page 173 for guidance, if necessary. To create a four-layer cake, split each cake layer in half horizontally, following the procedure on page 173. Drizzle 2 tablespoons strawberry puree over one layer and spread it around with the back of a spoon to encourage it to soak into the cake. Smoothly spread $\frac{1}{2}$ cup buttercream on top of the puree, and then add the second cake layer. Repeat the application of the puree and buttercream on the second and third layers, and then frost the top and sides of the cake with the buttercream.

To create the fresh berry garnish, slice the strawberries and arrange them on the top of the cake in a decorative pattern. For a simple garnish, use a cluster of whole berries in the center of the cake and some clusters around the base. For a fancier treatment, arrange sliced berries in a series of overlapping concentric circles (starting from the edge of the cake and working in toward the center). It should look like a flower with strawberry petals.

You can store the finished cake in an airtight container (or tented in plastic wrap) at room temperature for 1 to 2 days or in the refrigerator for 5 to 7 days. Or the cake layers can be frozen prior to filling and icing; wrap tightly in a double layer of plastic wrap and freeze up to 2 months. Thaw at room temperature before removing the plastic and filling and icing the cake.

I've iced this sophisticated take on an old-fashioned favorite with a dark and glossy ganache. But don't worry, the quintessential flavors are all there: chocolate, caramel, shredded coconut, and pecans.

German Chocolate Cake

Preheat the oven to 350°F. Lightly oil two 8-inch-diameter cake pans and pour the batter into the prepared cake pans. Bake in the center of the oven for 35 to 40 minutes. Cool the cakes on a wire rack for 10 minutes or until the pans are cool enough to handle safely, and then invert the cakes onto the rack to cool completely. Allowing the cakes to cool completely in the pans will result in cakes with soggy bottoms. While the cakes bake and cool, make the filling and ganache.

To make the filling: Combine the coconut milk, honey, and salt in a heavy-bottomed medium saucepan. (Use a pan that's larger than you think you'll need, as the caramel may bubble up vigorously; see Tip, page 60). Bring the mixture to a boil over medium-high heat, stirring constantly with a long-handled whisk or wooden spoon. Continue boiling, stirring continuously and carefully (the caramel is hot!), until the caramel darkens in color and thickens, about 15 minutes.

Remove the caramel from the heat and let cool for about 10 minutes. Pour into a clean bowl and cool for about 15 minutes more. Using a rubber spatula, fold in the coconut and pecans until thoroughly incorporated. The filling can be stored in the refrigerator in an airtight container up to 1 week. It will thicken up when chilled, so bring it to room temperature before using.

To assemble a two-layer cake, spread 1 cup of the filling between the layers, and then generously ice the top and sides of the cake with the ganache, referring to page 173 for guidance, if necessary. To create a four-layer cake, split each cake layer in half horizontally, following the procedure on page 173. Spread $\frac{1}{2}$ cup of the filling between each layer, and then generously ice the top and sides of the cake with the ganache. Press the toasted coconut onto the sides of the iced cake.

MAKES TWO 8-INCH-DIAMETER LAYERS (12 TO 16 SERVINGS)

Chocolate Cake batter (page 63)

COCONUT PECAN CARAMEL FILLING

3 cups canned unsweetened coconut milk (shake cans before opening)

1½ cups raw honey or organic cane sugar

1 teaspoon fine sea salt

1 cup unsweetened shredded coconut

1 cup chopped pecans

Chocolate Ganache (page 162)

1½ cups unsweetened shredded coconut, toasted (see page 195)

YELLOW CAKE

2¼ cups Gluten-Free All-
Purpose Flour Blend (page 191)

2 teaspoons baking powder

1 teaspoon baking soda

1 teaspoon xanthan gum

½ teaspoon fine sea salt

1 cup milk or unsweetened
coconut milk (from a carton)

1 tablespoon pure vanilla extract

1¼ cups organic cane sugar

⅔ cup organic mayonnaise

4 eggs (no substitutes possible
here), at room temperature

Pastry Cream (page 166)

Chocolate Ganache (page 162)

Boston Cream Pie is in fact not a pie at all. It consists of layers of golden sponge cake sandwiched with a pastry-cream filling and slathered with chocolate ganache. Mayonnaise replaces the butter (and adds extra egg), resulting in a cake that is moist and rich. Whether you choose to make a two- or four-layer version, the pastry cream oozes out irresistibly from the sides. That plus the thick chocolate glaze will have you scrambling for your fork.

Boston Cream Pie

Preheat the oven to 350°F. Lightly oil two 8-inch-diameter cake pans with nonstick cooking spray or coconut oil.

To make the cake: In a medium bowl, whisk together the flour blend, baking powder, baking soda, xanthan gum, and salt. In a small bowl, stir together the milk and vanilla extract. Set both bowls aside.

In the bowl of a stand mixer with the paddle attachment, beat the sugar and mayonnaise on medium speed until well combined. Scrape down the bowl. While beating on low, slowly add the eggs, one at a time. Then, increase the speed to medium and beat for 30 seconds. Scrape down the bowl.

Add one-fourth of the flour mixture to the egg mixture and beat on low until almost fully incorporated. Add one-third of the milk mixture and beat on low until almost fully incorporated. Repeat with the remaining flour and milk mixtures, starting and ending with the flour. When all the ingredients have been added, scrape down the bowl and beat on medium for 15 seconds.

Pour the batter into the prepared cake pans. Bake in the center of the oven for 25 minutes, or until the tops are golden brown and a toothpick inserted tests clean. Transfer the cakes to a wire rack to cool for 10 minutes, and then invert the cakes onto the rack to cool completely.

While the cakes bake and cool, make the pastry cream and ganache and set both aside until ready to assemble the cake. You can make the pastry cream and ganache up to 2 days in advance and refrigerate separately in airtight containers. If made ahead, bring the ganache to room temperature before assembly.

To assemble a two-layer cake, spread ¾ cup pastry cream between the layers. To create a four-layer cake, split each cake layer in half horizontally (see page 173). Spread a scant ½ cup pastry cream between each layer.

Place the cake on a wire rack with a baking sheet underneath, and then pour the ganache over the cake. Use an offset spatula to encourage the ganache to spread over the top of the cake and drip down the sides. Allow the ganache to set for about 30 minutes before serving.

CARROT CAKE

3 cups Gluten-Free Whole
Grain Flour Blend (page 191)

¼ cup flaxseed (optional)

1½ teaspoons xanthan gum

2 teaspoons baking soda

2 teaspoons baking powder

2 teaspoons ground cinnamon

1 teaspoon ground nutmeg

1 teaspoon fine sea salt

1 cup organic cane sugar

1 cup lightly packed dark
brown sugar

1 cup melted and cooled virgin
coconut oil (see page 193)

½ cup canned unsweetened
coconut milk (shake can before
opening)

4 eggs or Flax Egg Replacer
(page 194)

1 tablespoon pure vanilla extract

2 cups (about 12 ounces) peeled
and shredded carrots

1½ cups toasted chopped walnuts
(see page 195)

1 cup unsweetened shredded
coconut, toasted (see page 195)

Brown Sugar and Cinnamon
Cream Cheese Icing (page 165)

½ cup toasted walnuts, for
garnish (see page 195)

I know, I know, every baker has a beloved carrot cake recipe, but this one is truly divine. The gluten-free cake crumb is supermoist, and the flaxseed and walnuts add interesting textural contrast. The addition of brown sugar and cinnamon to the buttercream creates a harmonious balance between the cake and the filling. This cake freezes beautifully up to one month—just make sure you wrap it airtight in plastic wrap and keep it wrapped until completely thawed.

Carrot Cake with Brown Sugar
and Cinnamon Cream Cheese Icing

Preheat the oven to 350°F. Lightly oil two 8-inch-diameter cake pans with nonstick cooking spray or coconut oil.

To make the cake: In a medium bowl, whisk together the flour blend, flaxseed, xanthan gum, baking soda, baking powder, cinnamon, nutmeg, and salt. Set aside.

In the bowl of a stand mixer with the paddle attachment, combine the cane sugar, brown sugar, coconut oil, and coconut milk. Beat on low speed for 30 seconds to combine. Crack the eggs into the bowl, add the vanilla, and beat on medium for 20 seconds.

Add the flour mixture to the sugar mixture in two batches, beating on low after each addition until well combined. Scrape down the bowl with a rubber spatula. After all the flour mixture has been added, mix on medium for 20 seconds. Fold in the carrots along with the toasted walnuts and coconut, using a rubber spatula to evenly distribute the add-ins.

Pour the batter into the prepared cake pans. Bake in the center of the oven for 40 to 45 minutes, or until the tops are light golden and a toothpick inserted into the center tests clean. Cool the cakes on a wire rack for 15 minutes or until the pans are cool enough to handle safely, and then invert the cakes onto the rack to cool completely. Allowing the cakes to cool completely in the pans will result in cakes with soggy bottoms. Meanwhile, make the icing.

To assemble a two-layer cake, spread ¾ cup icing between the layers and on the top of the cake, and then generously ice the sides, referring to the instructions on page 173 for guidance, if necessary. To create a four-layer cake, split each cake layer in half horizontally, following the procedure on page 173. Spread ½ cup icing between each layer and on top of the cake, and then generously ice the sides. Sprinkle the toasted walnuts around the top edge of the cake to garnish.

Instead of incorporating the traditional walnuts or pecans, I ice this cake with almond buttercream and garnish it with slivered almonds. The pure almond extract in the buttercream marries perfectly with the warmth of the cinnamon, nutmeg, and pumpkin pie spice in the cake, taking this dessert to new flavor heights.

Cinnamon Spice Cake
with Almond Buttercream

Preheat the oven to 350°F. Lightly oil two 8-inch-diameter cake pans with nonstick cooking spray or coconut oil.

To make the cake: In a medium bowl, whisk together the flour blend, baking powder, cinnamon, xanthan gum, nutmeg, pumpkin pie spice, and salt. In a small bowl, mix together the milk and vanilla. Set both bowls aside.

In the bowl of a stand mixer with the paddle attachment, beat the butter and sugar on medium speed for 2 minutes or until light and fluffy. Scrape down the bowl with a rubber spatula. While beating on low, slowly add the egg whites. When all the whites have been added, increase the speed to medium and beat for 30 seconds. Scrape down the bowl.

Add one-fourth of the flour mixture to the butter mixture and mix on low speed until almost fully incorporated. Add about one-third of the milk mixture and mix on low speed until almost fully incorporated. Repeat with the remaining flour and milk mixtures, starting and ending with the flour. When all the ingredients have been added, scrape down the bowl and beat on medium for 15 seconds.

Pour the batter into the prepared cake pans. Bake in the center of the oven for 30 to 35 minutes, until the tops are light golden and a toothpick inserted into the center tests clean. Cool the cakes on a wire rack for 10 minutes or until the pans are cool enough to handle safely, and then invert the cakes onto the rack to cool completely. Allowing the cakes to cool completely in the pans will result in cakes with soggy bottoms. Meanwhile, make the buttercream.

To assemble a two-layer cake, spread ¾ cup buttercream between the layers and on the top of the cake, and then generously frost the sides. To create a four-layer cake, split each cake layer in half horizontally, following the procedure on page 173. Spread ½ cup buttercream between each layer and on top of the cake, and then generously frost the sides. Sprinkle the slivered almonds around the top edge of the cake.

CINNAMON SPICE CAKE

3 cups Gluten-Free All-Purpose Flour Blend (page 191)

2 teaspoons baking powder

2 teaspoons ground cinnamon

1½ teaspoons xanthan gum

1 teaspoon ground nutmeg

1 teaspoon pumpkin pie spice

½ teaspoon fine sea salt

1 cup milk or unsweetened coconut milk (from a carton), at room temperature

1 tablespoon pure vanilla extract

¾ cup (1½ sticks) unsalted butter or Earth Balance Buttery Sticks, at room temperature

1½ cups organic cane sugar

¾ cup egg whites (about 6 large whites), at room temperature

Almond Buttercream (page 156)

½ cup slivered almonds, for garnish

White Cake batter (page 44)

CARAMEL FILLING

1½ cups heavy cream or canned
unsweetened coconut milk

¾ cup organic cane sugar

½ teaspoon fine sea salt

Caramel Buttercream
(page 157)

This tender cake is slathered inside and out with the rich, intense taste of caramel. The gooey mmm-yum caramel filling provides richness and adds a satisfying textural contrast to the cake. I like to adorn the top of this cake with piped star pikes (for instructions, see page 177) and drizzle any extra caramel filling over the top.

Caramel Cream Cake

Preheat the oven to 350°F. Lightly oil two 8-inch-diameter cake pans and pour the batter into the prepared pans. Bake the cakes for 35 to 40 minutes, until the tops are light golden and a toothpick inserted into the center tests clean. Cool the cakes on a wire rack for 10 minutes or until the pans are cool enough to handle safely, and then invert the cakes onto the rack to cool completely. Allowing the cakes to cool completely in the pans will result in cakes with soggy bottoms.

While the cakes bake and cool, make the filling: Combine the cream, sugar, and salt in a heavy-bottomed medium saucepan. Use a pan that's larger than you think you'll need, as the caramel may bubble up vigorously. Bring the cream and sugar mixture to a boil over medium-high heat, stirring occasionally with a long-handled whisk or wooden spoon. Continue boiling and stirring carefully until the caramel darkens in color and thickens, about 15 minutes. Remove the caramel from the heat and let cool for about 10 minutes. Pour it into a clean bowl and cool completely. Then, make the buttercream.

To assemble a two-layer cake, use half the caramel filling between the layers, and then generously frost the sides and top of the cake with the buttercream, referring to page 173 for guidance, if necessary. To create a four-layer cake, split each cake layer in half horizontally, following the procedure on page 173. Use one-third of the caramel filling between each layer, and then generously frost the sides and top of the cake.

You can freeze the unfrosted cake layers, each tightly wrapped in a double layer of plastic wrap, up to 1 month; thaw at room temperature before removing the plastic and filling and icing the cake.

TIP

Be very cautious when making the caramel. Boiling sugar is extremely hot and will burn you badly if it splatters. Keep the caramel moving so it doesn't burn on the bottom, but be gentle so you don't splash it on yourself. A long-handled whisk is the perfect tool, but a flat wooden spoon or heatproof spatula works well, too. This is *not* a task to share with kids!

Pour a tall glass of milk and pull up a chair: you're going to want to linger over this one. My classic chocolate layer cake is old-fashioned goodness at its unpretentious best. I add a little coffee to the cake batter. You won't detect the coffee flavor, but this addition rounds out and enhances the chocolate flavor. Slather on the rich chocolate buttercream and you have a chocolate lover's delight. To complete the ruffled ribbon icing technique (see page 180 for instructions), you'll need to triple the buttercream recipe.

Chocolate Layer Cake

To make the cake: Preheat the oven to 350°F. Lightly oil two 8-inch-diameter cake pans with nonstick cooking spray or coconut oil.

In the bowl of a stand mixer fitted with the paddle attachment, combine the flour blend, sugar, cocoa powder, baking powder, baking soda, xanthan gum, and salt. Mix on low speed to thoroughly combine.

In a medium bowl, combine the eggs, milk, coconut oil, and vanilla, whisking lightly just to combine. Add the egg mixture to the flour mixture and mix on low for 30 seconds. Scrape down the bowl with a rubber spatula, and then mix on medium-low for 1 minute. Pour the coffee into the batter and mix on low for 30 seconds just to combine, and then on medium-low for 30 seconds more or until well combined and smooth. The batter will be on the thin side and easy to pour.

Pour the batter into the prepared cake pans. Bake in the center of the oven for 30 to 35 minutes, or until a toothpick inserted into the center tests clean. Cool the cakes on a wire rack for 10 minutes or until the pans are cool enough to handle, and then invert the cakes onto the rack to cool. Allowing the cakes to cool completely in the pans will result in cakes with soggy bottoms. Meanwhile, make the buttercream.

To assemble a two-layer cake, spread ¾ cup buttercream between the layers and on the top of the cake, and then generously frost the sides, referring to the instructions on page 173. To create a four-layer cake, split each cake layer in half horizontally, following the procedure on page 173. Spread ½ cup buttercream between each layer and on top of the cake, and then generously frost the sides.

You can store the finished cake in an airtight container at room temperature (or tented in plastic wrap) for 1 to 2 days or in the refrigerator for 5 to 7 days. Or you can freeze the unfrosted cake layers, each tightly wrapped in a double layer of plastic wrap, up to 1 month; thaw at room temperature before removing the plastic and filling and frosting the cake.

CHOCOLATE CAKE

1¾ cups Gluten-Free Whole Grain Flour Blend (page 191)

2 cups organic cane sugar

1 cup natural (nonalkalized) cocoa powder

1½ teaspoons baking powder

1½ teaspoons baking soda

1 teaspoon xanthan gum

½ teaspoon fine sea salt

2 large eggs or Flax Egg Replacer (page 194)

1 cup milk or unsweetened coconut milk (from a carton)

½ cup melted and cooled virgin coconut oil (see page 193)

2 teaspoons pure vanilla extract

¾ cup hot coffee

Chocolate Buttercream (page 157)

MAKES TWO 8-INCH-DIAMETER
LAYERS (12 TO 16 SERVINGS)

1 cup chocolate chips
(milk, semisweet, or dark)

Chocolate Cake batter
(page 63)

Chocolate Peppermint Ganache
(page 163)

Peppermint Buttercream
(page 159)

12 red-and-white-striped
peppermint candies, chopped
or whole

Rich chocolate cake is studded with chocolate chips, filled with a smooth chocolate and peppermint ganache, and then slathered with a sweet and refreshing peppermint buttercream. Red and white peppermint candies dot the top—making this cake a festive centerpiece on a holiday buffet table. For an even fancier finish, use the petal icing technique; see instructions on page 177.

Chocolate Peppermint Cake
with Peppermint Buttercream

Preheat the oven to 350°F. Lightly oil two 8-inch-diameter cake pans. Fold the chocolate chips into the cake batter, using a rubber spatula to evenly distribute them. Pour the batter into the prepared cake pans. Bake in the center of the oven for 30 to 35 minutes, or until a toothpick inserted tests clean. Cool the cakes on a wire rack for 10 minutes or until the pans are cool enough to handle, and then invert the cakes onto the rack to cool completely. Meanwhile, make the buttercream.

To assemble a two-layer cake, spread 1 cup of the ganache between the cake layers, and then generously frost the top and sides of the cake with the buttercream, referring to page 173 for guidance. To create a four-layer cake, split each cake layer in half horizontally, following the procedure on page 173. Spread $\frac{1}{2}$ cup ganache between each cake layer, and then generously frost the top and sides of the cake with the buttercream. Sprinkle the top of the cake with crushed or whole peppermint candies.

You can store the finished cake in an airtight container at room temperature (or tented in plastic wrap) for 1 to 2 days or in the refrigerator for 5 to 7 days. Or you can freeze the un-iced cake layers, each tightly wrapped in a double layer of plastic wrap, up to 1 month; thaw at room temperature before removing the plastic and filling and icing the cake.

Petal icing technique (see page 177) shown on Chocolate Peppermint Cake (page 64)

3

CUPCAKES
— *filled & frosted* —

About two decades ago, the world went cuckoo for cupcakes, and it's a mad affair that continues to flourish. After all, what's not to love about these tender little cakelets, beckoning you with their seductive whirls of buttercream? It's enough to make anyone swoon. But if you thought the passion couldn't get any more intense, I have a surprise for you . . .

Many of my cupcakes contain a luscious, creamy filling in the middle, so you get a delightfully sweet surprise when you take your first bite. The cake, icing, and filling (and sometimes a garnish) all work in concert to make you even more crazy about cupcakes than you were when you first met them. I call the bits of cake you remove to make room for the filling "cake bellies." They're great for snacking, or you can layer the cake bellies with whipped cream and fresh fruit to make a quick trifle.

Each recipe makes two dozen cupcakes, but you can easily halve the yields if you choose. The cupcakes, prior to filling and frosting, can be stored in an airtight container and frozen for up to 1 month. The paper cups tend to fall off during the thawing process, but you can serve the cupcakes without or just replace the cups.

You can store the frosted (or filled and frosted) cupcakes in an airtight container, in a single layer, at room temperature for 1 to 2 days or in the refrigerator for 5 to 7 days. Or, prior to filling and frosting, you can freeze the cupcakes in an airtight container up to 1 month; thaw at room temperature before filling and frosting. If the cupcakes are garnished, add the garnish just before serving.

Now you can enjoy this sensational summer dessert in cupcake form. My Very Vanilla Cake (page 40) and this strawberry buttercream make perfect gluten-free stand-ins for the traditional components, bringing all the flavors together in a portable, finger-licking treat.

Strawberry Shortcake Cupcakes

Preheat the oven to 350°F. Line a 24-cup cupcake pan (or two 12-cup cupcake pans) with cupcake liners.

Pour the batter into the prepared cupcake pans, filling them about three-fourths full. Bake in the center of the oven for about 20 minutes, until the tops are light golden and a toothpick inserted into the center of a cupcake tests clean. Let the cupcakes cool completely on a wire rack before removing them from the pan, referring to page 172 for guidance, if necessary.

While the cupcakes bake and cool, make the buttercream: In the bowl of a stand mixer with the paddle attachment, beat the butter on high for 1 minute or until well whipped. Add the confectioners' sugar, cover most of your bowl with a kitchen towel to avoid a dust storm, and beat on low for 1 minute to combine. Add the vanilla and salt and combine on low, then beat on medium for 30 seconds more or until whipped and smooth. You can refrigerate the buttercream in an airtight container for 5 days or freeze for 1 month. Bring to room temperature and beat in the bowl of a stand mixer to restore the proper texture before using.

When you're ready to proceed, gently fold the chopped strawberries into the buttercream; they will bleed, creating a lovely pink hue. Frost the tops of the cupcakes with the buttercream, referring to page 174 for guidance. Just before serving, top each cupcake with fresh strawberry, either whole or cut in slices.

Very Vanilla Cake batter (page 40)

FRESH STRAWBERRY BUTTERCREAM

1 cup (2 sticks) unsalted butter or nonhydrogenated vegetable shortening, at room temperature

3¾ cups confectioners' sugar (to make your own, see page 192)

1 teaspoon pure vanilla extract

½ teaspoon fine sea salt

1 cup finely chopped fresh strawberries or frozen strawberries, thawed

24 fresh strawberries, for garnish

White Cake batter (page 44)

Pastry Cream (page 166)

Chocolate Ganache (page 162)

2 ripe bananas, coarsely chopped

Chocolate and banana make a yummy duo, loved by kids and the kid in all of us. Here, the two are brought together in a cupcake reminiscent of a chocolate-topped banana cream pie. If you want to crown your cupcakes with lavish quantities of chocolate ganache, see the instructions on page 177 for making the round cupcake mounds shown here.

Banana Cream Cupcakes
with Chocolate Ganache

Preheat the oven to 350°F. Line a 24-cup cupcake pan (or two 12-cup cupcake pans) with cupcake liners.

Pour the batter into the prepared cupcake pans, filling them about three-fourths full. Bake in the center of the oven for about 20 minutes, until the tops are light golden and a toothpick inserted into the center of a cupcake tests clean. Let the cupcakes cool completely on a wire rack before removing them from the pan, referring to page 172 for guidance, if necessary.

While the cupcakes bake and cool, make the pastry cream and ganache. You can refrigerate the ganache in an airtight container for up to 1 week. Bring to room temperature before using.

When you're ready to assemble the cupcakes, remove the center of each cupcake with a paring knife, referring to page 174 for guidance. Fill each hole with about 1 tablespoon pastry cream (a spoon will do the job). Press 1 tablespoon of chopped banana into the cream, and then ice the cupcakes with the chocolate ganache, referring to page 174 for guidance, if necessary.

VARIATION: Chocolate Peanut Butter Banana Cupcakes

Make and bake the cupcakes and prepare the ganache and coarsely chopped bananas as instructed. (Omit the pastry cream; you will use the ganache and chopped bananas for the filling.) Make Peanut Butter Buttercream (page 161) for the icing. Fill the cupcakes with the ganache and chopped bananas and ice the tops with the buttercream.

White Cake batter (page 44)

Peanut Butter Buttercream
(page 161)

1¾ cups natural jelly, jam,
or preserves of choice

What's better than a peanut butter and jelly sandwich? This recipe: tender vanilla cupcakes filled with your choice of jelly and slathered with a creamy peanut butter frosting. It's a nostalgic treat that will transport you back to childhood. If you're making these cupcakes for someone with peanut allergies, feel free to substitute almond or cashew butter—or any other nut butter you'd like.

Peanut Butter and Jelly Cupcakes

Preheat the oven to 350°F. Line a 24-cup cupcake pan (or two 12-cup cupcake pans) with cupcake liners.

Pour the batter into the prepared cupcake pans, filling them about three-fourths full. Bake in the center of the oven for about 20 minutes, until the tops are light golden and a toothpick inserted into the center of a cupcake tests clean. Let the cupcakes cool completely on a wire rack before removing them from the pan, referring to page 172 for guidance, if necessary.

While the cupcakes bake and cool, prepare the buttercream.

When you're ready to assemble the cupcakes, remove the center of each cupcake (see page 174 for guidance). Fill each hole with 1 to 2 tablespoons jelly (a spoon will do the job), and then frost the tops of the cupcakes with buttercream (see page 174 for guidance). Top each cupcake with a small spoonful of jelly.

I created this extravaganza of a cupcake for the grand opening party of my bakery, loading chocolate into the cake, filling, frosting, and garnish. The varying textures of the chocolaty elements are sure to dazzle the taste buds of even the most devoted chocolate lover. Have fun with the garnish and make it your own: from shaved or grated chocolate to chocolate sprinkles or a drizzle of ganache, there are lots of decadent options.

Chocolate Obsession Cupcakes

MAKES 2 DOZEN CUPCAKES

Chocolate Cake batter (page 63)

Chocolate Ganache (page 162)

Chocolate Ganache Buttercream (page 157)

½ cup shaved or grated chocolate, 2 tablespoons chocolate sprinkles, or ¼ cup Chocolate Ganache (page 162), for garnish

Preheat the oven to 350°F. Line a 24-cup cupcake pan (or two 12-cup cupcake pans) with cupcake liners.

Pour the batter into the prepared cupcake pans, filling them about three-fourths full. Bake in the center of the oven for about 20 minutes, until the center of a cupcake bounces back when pressed lightly and a toothpick inserted into the center tests clean. Let the cupcakes cool completely on a wire rack before removing them from the pan, referring to page 172 for guidance, if necessary.

While the cupcakes bake and cool, make the ganache, reserving $\frac{1}{4}$ cup for the buttercream. When the reserved ganache is cool, make the buttercream.

When you're ready to assemble the cupcakes, remove the center of each cupcake, referring to page 174 for guidance. Fill each hole with 1 to 2 tablespoons ganache (a spoon will do the job), and then frost the tops of the cupcakes with the buttercream, referring to page 174 for guidance, if necessary. Top the cupcakes with your chocolate garnish of choice (see page 182)—or with several!

VARIATION: Rocky Road Cupcakes

Make and bake the chocolate cupcakes and prepare the Chocolate Ganache. Prepare Swiss Meringue Icing (page 165). When you're ready to assemble the cupcakes, fill them with the ganache and ice them with the meringue. Instead of shaved chocolate, garnish each cupcake with a pecan half.

You get a double whammy of salted caramel here by using it in both the filling and the icing. Try garnishing these cupcakes with a tiny pinch of pink Himalayan salt—the pale pink color is lovely against the buttercream.

Salted Caramel and Apple Cupcakes

CINNAMON CUPCAKES

3 cups Gluten-Free All-Purpose Flour Blend (page 191)

2 teaspoons baking powder

2 teaspoons ground cinnamon

1½ teaspoons xanthan gum

½ teaspoon fine sea salt

1 cup milk or unsweetened coconut milk (from a carton), at room temperature

1 tablespoon pure vanilla extract

1 teaspoon vanilla bean paste (see page 196; optional)

¾ cup (1½ sticks) unsalted butter or Earth Balance Vegan Buttery Sticks, at room temperature

1½ cups organic cane sugar

¾ cup egg whites (about 6 large whites), at room temperature

SALTED CARAMEL AND APPLE FILLING

1½ cups heavy cream or canned unsweetened coconut milk

¾ cup organic cane sugar

1 teaspoon fine sea salt

2 Granny Smith apples, peeled, cored, and finely chopped

Salted Caramel Buttercream (page 161)

Pinch of Himalayan pink sea salt, for garnish (optional)

Preheat the oven to 350°F. Line a 24-cup cupcake pan (or two 12-cup cupcake pans) with cupcake liners.

To make the cupcakes: In a medium bowl, whisk together the flour blend, baking powder, cinnamon, xanthan gum, and salt. In a small bowl, combine the milk, vanilla extract, and vanilla bean paste. Set both bowls aside.

In the bowl of a stand mixer with the paddle attachment, beat the butter and sugar on medium speed for 2 minutes, or until light and fluffy. Scrape down the bowl. While beating on low, slowly add the egg whites. When all the whites have been added, increase the speed to medium and beat for 30 seconds. Scrape down the bowl.

Add one-fourth of the flour mixture to the butter mixture and beat on low until almost fully incorporated. Add one-third of the milk mixture and beat on low until almost fully incorporated. Repeat with the remaining flour and milk mixtures, starting and ending with the flour. When all the ingredients have been added, scrape down the bowl and beat on medium for 15 seconds.

Pour the batter into the prepared cupcake pans, filling them about three-fourths full. Bake in the center of the oven for about 20 minutes, until the tops are light golden and a toothpick inserted into the center of a cupcake tests clean. Let the cupcakes cool completely on a wire rack before removing them from the pan.

While the cupcakes bake and cool, make the filling: Combine the cream, sugar, and salt in a heavy-bottomed saucepan. Use a larger pan than you think you'll need, as the caramel may bubble vigorously (see Tip, page 60). Bring the cream and sugar mixture to a boil over medium-high heat, stirring occasionally. Continue boiling, stirring carefully, until the caramel darkens in color and thickens, about 15 minutes.

Remove the caramel from the heat and let cool for about 10 minutes. Reserve 2 tablespoons of the caramel for the buttercream. Add the chopped apples to the remaining caramel, stirring to combine. Pour the salted caramel and apple filling into a heatproof container to cool completely. Meanwhile, make the buttercream.

When you're ready to assemble the cupcakes, remove the center of each cupcake, referring to page 174 for guidance. Fill each hole with 1 to 2 tablespoons caramel-apple filling, and then frost the tops of the cupcakes with caramel buttercream, referring to page 174 for guidance, if necessary. Sprinkle each cupcake with a pinch of the pink sea salt, or just a single large crystal.

ESPRESSO CHOCOLATE CUPCAKES

2 cups organic cane sugar

1¾ cups Gluten-Free Whole Grain Flour Blend (page 191)

1 cup natural (nonalkalized) cocoa powder

1½ teaspoons baking powder

1½ teaspoons baking soda

1 teaspoon xanthan gum

½ teaspoon fine sea salt

2 eggs or Flax Egg Replacer (page 194)

1 cup milk or unsweetened coconut milk (from a carton), at room temperature

½ cup melted and cooled virgin coconut oil (see page 193)

2 teaspoons pure vanilla extract

¾ cup hot coffee

1 tablespoon instant espresso powder

Espresso Buttercream (page 159)

Chocolate-covered espresso beans, for garnish (optional)

If you love mocha, that divine cupful of chocolate and espresso with a froth of milk on top, then this cupcake is for you. You'll get a triple dose of coffee and espresso from the cake, the buttercream, and, if you like, the chocolate-covered espresso bean on top. For a stunning presentation, frost these cupcakes using the dot technique (see page 175 for guidance), but don't press down the little tail on top of your dot.

Mocha Latte Cupcakes

Preheat the oven to 350°F. Line a 24-cup cupcake pan (or two 12-cup cupcake pans) with cupcake liners.

To make the cupcakes: In the bowl of a stand mixer with the paddle attachment, combine the sugar, flour blend, cocoa powder, baking powder, baking soda, xanthan gum, and salt. Mix on low to thoroughly combine.

In a medium bowl, combine the eggs, milk, coconut oil, and vanilla, whisking lightly just to combine. Add the egg mixture to the flour mixture and beat on low for 30 seconds. Scrape down the bowl with a rubber spatula, and then mix on medium-low for 1 minute. Whisk together the hot coffee and espresso powder. Pour the coffee mixture into the batter and mix on low for 30 seconds just to combine, and then on medium-low for 30 seconds more or until well combined and smooth. The batter will be on the thin side and easy to pour.

Pour the batter into the prepared cupcake pans, filling them about three-fourths full. Bake in the center of the oven for about 20 minutes, until the center of a cupcake springs back when lightly pressed and a toothpick inserted into the cupcake tests clean. Let the cupcakes cool completely on a wire rack before removing them from the pan, referring to page 172 for guidance, if necessary.

While the cupcakes bake and cool, make the buttercream. Ice the tops of the cupcakes with the buttercream, referring to page 174 for guidance, if necessary. Top each cupcake with a chocolate-covered espresso bean, if you wish.

Chocolate flavored with cinnamon and chiles is a delectable combo that's as old as the Aztecs—and a beloved trio in Southwestern cuisine. Layering ancho and cinnamon flavors in the cake, the ganache, and even the garnish delivers a more rounded taste. While the flavors are subtle in the baked cake, the raw spices in the ganache can be more potent. I provide a measurement range so you can adjust the spices to suit your heat tolerance. To create the perfect base for a dusting of ground cinnamon and ancho chile powder, pipe a star swirl of frosting onto each cupcake (see page 179 for instructions).

Ancho Chile, Chocolate, and Cinnamon Cupcakes

Preheat the oven to 350°F. Line a 24-cup cupcake pan (or two 12-cup cupcake pans) with cupcake liners.

To make the cupcakes: In the bowl of a stand mixer with the paddle attachment, combine the sugar, flour blend, cocoa powder, cinnamon, chile powder, baking powder, baking soda, xanthan gum, and salt. Mix on low to thoroughly combine.

In a medium bowl, combine the eggs, milk, coconut oil, and vanilla, whisking lightly just to combine. Add the egg mixture to the flour mixer and beat on low for 30 seconds. Scrape down the bowl with a rubber spatula, then mix on medium-low for 1 minute. Pour in the hot coffee and mix on low for 30 seconds just to combine, and then on medium-low for 30 seconds more or until well combined and smooth. The batter will be on the thin side and easy to pour.

Pour the batter into the prepared cupcake pans, filling them about three-fourths full. Bake in the center of the oven for about 20 minutes, until the center of a cupcake springs back when lightly pressed and a toothpick inserted into the center tests clean. Let the cupcakes cool completely on a wire rack before removing them from the pan, referring to page 172 for guidance, if necessary. Meanwhile, prepare the ganache and buttercream.

When you're ready to assemble the cupcakes, remove the center of each cupcake, referring to page 174 for guidance. Fill each hole with 1 to 2 tablespoons of the ganache (a spoon will do the job), then frost the tops of the cupcakes with the buttercream, referring to page 174 for guidance, if necessary. Using a fine-mesh sieve or flour sifter, lightly dust the cupcakes with the cinnamon and chile powder.

ANCHO CINNAMON CUPCAKES

2 cups organic cane sugar

1¾ cups Gluten-Free Whole Grain Flour Blend (page 191)

1 cup natural (nonalkalized) cocoa powder

2 teaspoons ground cinnamon

2 teaspoons ancho chile powder

1½ teaspoons baking powder

1½ teaspoons baking soda

1 teaspoon xanthan gum

½ teaspoon fine sea salt

2 eggs or Flax Egg Replacer (page 194)

1 cup milk or unsweetened coconut milk (from a carton), at room temperature

½ cup melted and cooled virgin coconut oil (see page 193)

2 teaspoons pure vanilla extract

¾ cup hot coffee

Ancho Cinnamon Ganache (page 162)

Very Vanilla Buttercream (page 161)

Ground cinnamon and ancho chile powder, for dusting

Star swirl frosting technique (see page 179) shown on Ancho Chile, Chocolate, and Cinnamon Cupcakes (page 83)

Chocolate Cake batter
(page 63)

Chocolate Hazelnut Ganache
(page 163)

Chocolate Hazelnut Buttercream
(page 158)

24 whole peeled, toasted
hazelnuts, for garnish (see page
195)

This one is for my son, Cade, who absolutely adores Nutella. The chocolaty
hazelnut spread features prominently in the filling as well as in the frosting,
delivering a double dose of its rich, nutty flavor in every bite. Cade acted as my
lead taste tester on the development of this recipe—and he's quite the chocolate
cupcake aficionado—so you can be sure this one's a winner.

Chocolate Hazelnut Cupcakes

Preheat the oven to 350°F. Line a 24-cup cupcake pan (or two 12-cup cupcake pans)
with cupcake liners.

Pour the batter into the prepared cupcake pans, filling them about three-fourths full.
Bake in the center of the oven for about 20 minutes, until the center of a cupcake
springs back when lightly pressed and a toothpick inserted into the center tests clean.
Let the cupcakes cool completely on a wire rack before removing them from the pan,
referring to page 172 for guidance, if necessary.

While the cupcakes bake and cool, make the ganache and buttercream.

When you're ready to assemble the cupcakes, remove the center of each cupcake,
referring to page 174 for guidance. Fill each hole with 1 to 2 tablespoons of the
ganache (a spoon will do the job), and then frost the tops of the cupcakes with the
buttercream, referring to page 174 for guidance, if necessary. Top each cupcake
with a toasted hazelnut.

Would you like cupcakes, cheesecake, or chocolate? Silly question—of course you want them all! You'll be using freshly squeezed orange juice in all the components of these cupcakes, so start your prep by squeezing 1 or 2 oranges and then measuring out what you need as you move through the steps.

Orange-Chocolate Cheesecake Cupcakes

Preheat the oven to 350°F. Line a 24-cup cupcake pan (or two 12-cup cupcake pans) with cupcake liners.

To make the cupcakes: In a medium bowl, whisk together the flour blend, orange zest, baking powder, xanthan gum, and salt. In a small bowl, mix the milk, orange juice, and vanilla. Set both bowls aside.

In the bowl of a stand mixer with a paddle attachment, beat the butter and both sugars on medium speed for 2 minutes, or until light and fluffy. Scrape down the bowl with a rubber spatula. While beating on low, slowly add the egg whites. When all the whites have been added, increase the speed to medium and beat for 30 seconds. Scrape down the bowl.

Add one-fourth of the flour mixture to the butter mixture and beat on low until almost fully incorporated. Add one-third of the milk mixture and beat on low to incorporate. Repeat with the remaining flour and milk mixtures, starting and ending with the flour. When all the ingredients have been added, scrape down the bowl and beat on medium for 15 seconds. Pour the batter into the prepared cupcake pans, filling them about three-fourths full. Set aside while you make the cheesecake.

To make the cheesecake: In the bowl of a stand mixer with the paddle attachment, combine the cream cheese and sugar; beat on medium until smooth, about 3 minutes. Add the egg and the orange zest and juice; beat on medium until well combined. You don't want to whip a lot of air into this batter, just beat it until smooth.

Add about 1 tablespoon cheesecake batter to the cake batter in each cup of the cupcake pan, using a spoon to lightly swirl the two batters together. Bake in the center of the oven for 20 minutes, or until the cake is done (you can use a toothpick test) and the cheesecake is set but not dried out. Let the cupcakes cool completely on a wire rack before removing them from the pan, referring to page 172 for guidance, if necessary.

While the cupcakes bake and cool, make the ganache. Ice the top of each cupcake with a small amount of the ganache—it's rich!

You can refrigerate the cupcakes in an airtight container, in a single layer or in layers separated by waxed paper, for 5 to 7 days. (Do not freeze or store at room temperature.)

ORANGE CUPCAKES

3¼ cups Gluten-Free All-Purpose Flour Blend (page 191)

1 tablespoon organic orange zest

2 teaspoons baking powder

1½ teaspoons xanthan gum

½ teaspoon fine sea salt

1 cup milk or unsweetened coconut milk (from a carton), at room temperature

¼ cup freshly squeezed orange juice

2 teaspoons pure vanilla extract

¾ cup (1½ sticks) unsalted butter or Earth Balance Vegan Buttery Sticks, at room temperature

1 cup organic cane sugar

½ cup lightly packed dark brown sugar

¾ cup egg whites (about 6 large whites), at room temperature

ORANGE CHEESECAKE

8 ounces cream cheese or dairy-free cream cheese, at room temperature

½ cup organic cane sugar

1 egg

1 tablespoon organic orange zest

1 teaspoon freshly squeezed orange juice

Orange Chocolate Ganache (page 163)

PUMPKIN GINGER CUPCAKES

3 cups Gluten-Free Whole Grain Flour Blend (page 191)

1¾ cups organic cane sugar

1 teaspoon ground cinnamon

1 teaspoon baking soda

1 teaspoon xanthan gum

1 teaspoon peeled, finely grated fresh ginger

½ teaspoon fine sea salt

1¼ cups melted and cooled virgin coconut oil (see page 193)

3 large eggs or Flax Egg Replacer (page 194), at room temperature

1 cup milk or unsweetened coconut milk (from a carton)

1 cup canned pumpkin puree (*not* pumpkin pie filling)

2 teaspoons pure vanilla extract

CINNAMON CREAM CHEESE ICING

8 ounces cream cheese or dairy-free cream cheese, at room temperature

4 tablespoons unsalted butter or Earth Balance Vegan Buttery Stick, at room temperature

2½ cups confectioners' sugar (to make your own, see page 192)

2 teaspoons ground cinnamon

1 teaspoon pure vanilla extract

2 tablespoons chopped crystallized ginger, for garnish

The warm and spicy smell of these cupcakes in the oven is sure to trigger happy Thanksgiving and Christmas memories—but feel free to indulge in these pumpkin treats any time you like. Ginger is a wonderful complement to pumpkin. Use grated fresh ginger in the cake batter and spicy-sweet crystallized ginger for garnishing your goodies.

Pumpkin Ginger Cupcakes

Preheat the oven to 350°F. Line a 24-cup cupcake pan (or two 12-cup cupcake pans) with cupcake liners.

To make the cupcakes: In the bowl of a stand mixer, combine the flour blend, sugar, cinnamon, baking soda, xanthan gum, ginger, and salt. Mix on low speed to thoroughly combine. Add the coconut oil, eggs, milk, pumpkin, and vanilla to the flour mixture and mix on low for 30 seconds. Scrape down the bowl with a rubber spatula, then mix on medium for 30 seconds more or until well combined.

Pour the batter into the prepared cupcake pans, filling them about three-fourths full. Bake in the center of the oven for about 20 minutes, until the center of a cupcake bounces back when lightly pressed and a toothpick inserted into the center tests clean. Let the cupcakes cool completely on a wire rack before removing them from the pan, referring to page 172 for guidance, if necessary.

While the cupcakes bake and cool, make the icing: In the bowl of a stand mixer with the paddle attachment, beat the cream cheese and butter on high for 1 minute or until well whipped. Add the confectioners' sugar, cinnamon, and vanilla, cover most of your bowl with a kitchen towel to avoid a dust storm, and beat on low for 1 minute to combine. Beat on medium for 30 seconds, scrape down the bowl, then beat on medium for 1 minute more or until light and fluffy. You can refrigerate the icing in an airtight container for 5 days or freeze for 1 month. Bring to room temperature and beat in the bowl of a stand mixer to restore proper texture before using.

Ice the tops of the cupcakes with the cream cheese icing, referring to page 174 for guidance, if necessary. Just before serving, garnish each cupcake with the crystallized ginger.

Chocolate and cherry are a well-loved pairing—one that conjures up sweet delights like Black Forest cake and cherry cordials. Here, I've turned up the volume on this classic flavor combo by spiking the chocolate cake *and* the chocolate ganache icing with kirsch to create a grown-up cupcake that's decadent, rich, and oh-so-sophisticated. Just top with a cherry and serve. Many grain-based alcohols contain gluten, but kirsch, a clear brandy distilled from cherries and cherry pits, is gluten free.

Chocolate-Cherry Kirsch Cupcakes

Preheat the oven to 350°F. Line a 24-cup cupcake pan (or two 12-cup cupcake pans) with cupcake liners.

To make the cupcakes: In the bowl of a stand mixer, combine the sugar, flour blend, cocoa powder, baking powder, baking soda, xanthan gum, and salt. Mix on low speed to thoroughly combine.

In a medium bowl, combine the eggs, milk, coconut oil, and kirsch, whisking lightly just to combine. Add the egg mixture to the flour mixture and mix on low for 30 seconds. Scrape down the bowl with a rubber spatula, and then mix on medium-low for 1 minute. Pour the coffee into the batter; mix on low for 30 seconds just to combine, and then on medium-low for 30 seconds more or until well combined and smooth. The batter will be on the thin side and easy to pour.

Pour the batter into the prepared cupcake pans, filling them about three-fourths full. Bake in the center of the oven for about 20 minutes, until the center of a cupcake bounces back when lightly pressed and a toothpick inserted into the center tests clean. Let the cupcakes cool completely on a wire rack before removing them from the pan, referring to page 172 for guidance. Meanwhile, make the ganache.

Ice the tops of the cupcakes with the ganache, referring to page 174 for guidance, if necessary. Garnish each cupcake with one whole cherry.

CHOCOLATE CHERRY CUPCAKES

2 cups organic cane sugar

1¾ cups Gluten-Free Whole Grain Flour Blend (page 191)

1 cup natural (nonalkalized) cocoa powder

1½ teaspoons baking powder

1½ teaspoons baking soda

1 teaspoon xanthan gum

½ teaspoon fine sea salt

2 eggs or Flax Egg Replacer (page 194)

1 cup milk or unsweetened coconut milk (from a carton), at room temperature

½ cup melted and cooled virgin coconut oil (see page 193)

2 teaspoons kirsch

¾ cup hot coffee

Chocolate Cherry Ganache (page 162)

24 whole cherries with stems, for garnish

LEMON CURD

6 egg yolks (reserve the whites to use in the cake)

¾ cup organic cane sugar

⅓ cup freshly squeezed lemon juice

½ cup (1 stick) cold unsalted butter or Earth Balance Vegan Buttery Stick, cut into 16 cubes

Lemon Cake batter (page 38)

Swiss Meringue Icing (page 165)

My dad's favorite dessert was lemon meringue pie, so I transformed this classic southern pie into cupcakes in his honor. These cakes are tender and zesty, the lemon curd filling is divinely smooth and perfectly sweet-tart, and the meringue forms a gratifying froth on top. For meringue success, make sure that your bowl and whisk are free of any fats like oil or butter. Fats will keep the meringue from achieving full volume. Torching the meringue adds eye appeal but it's entirely optional. Your cupcakes will be just as scrumptious if you skip it.

Lemon Meringue Cupcakes

To make the lemon curd: Prepare a double boiler by pouring 2 inches of water into a small saucepan and placing a shallow stainless steel bowl atop the pan so that the bottom does not touch the water (you want indirect heat). Bring the water to a boil over high heat. In the top of the double boiler, whisk together the egg yolks, sugar, and lemon juice. Continue to whisk constantly until the sugar dissolves and the mixture thickens enough to coat the back of a spoon, 5 to 10 minutes. (Don't leave the egg-yolk mixture unattended over the double boiler; you must whisk constantly to avoid curdling or burning.) Remove from the heat and add the butter, two pieces at a time, whisking to melt. Allow each addition to melt almost completely before adding the next two pieces of butter. Pour the lemon curd into a clean bowl and cover with plastic wrap, pressing the plastic directly onto the surface of the curd to keep a skin from developing. Refrigerate until completely chilled and thickened, about 1 hour. The curd can be kept in the refrigerator, in an airtight container, up to 2 weeks.

Preheat the oven to 350°F. Line a 24-cup cupcake pan (or two 12-cup cupcake pans) with cupcake liners. Pour the batter into the prepared cupcake pans, filling them about three-fourths full. Bake in the center of the oven for about 20 minutes, until the tops are light golden and a toothpick inserted into the center of a cupcake tests clean. Let the cupcakes cool completely on a wire rack before removing them from the pan, referring to page 172 for guidance, if necessary.

Just before you're ready to assemble the cupcakes, make the meringue icing.

To assemble the cupcakes, remove the center of each cupcake, referring to page 174 for guidance. Fill each hole with 1 to 2 tablespoons lemon curd (a spoon will do the job), and then top the cupcakes with lemon meringue, referring to page 174 for guidance, if necessary. For a pastry chef–worthy finish, toast the meringue on each cupcake with a kitchen torch until it's nicely browned, focusing the flame on the peak of the icing (see page 187 for guidance).

LIME CURD

6 egg yolks (reserve the whites for the cake)

¾ cup organic cane sugar

⅓ cup freshly squeezed lime juice

½ cup (1 stick) cold unsalted butter or Earth Balance Vegan Buttery Stick, cut into 16 cubes

2 teaspoons high-quality tequila (such as Patrón; see Tip), or more to taste

TEQUILA LIME CUPCAKES

3 cups Gluten-Free All-Purpose Flour Blend (page 191)

2 teaspoons baking powder

1½ teaspoons xanthan gum

1 teaspoon organic lime zest

½ teaspoon fine sea salt

1 cup milk or unsweetened coconut milk (from a carton), at room temperature

1 tablespoon freshly squeezed lime juice

2 teaspoons high-quality tequila (such as Patrón)

¾ cup (1½ sticks) unsalted butter or Earth Balance Vegan Buttery Sticks, at room temperature

1½ cups organic cane sugar

¾ cup egg whites (about 6 large whites), at room temperature

These zingers boast lime in the cake, filling, and frosting and a sugary lime zest garnish. I created these tipsy treats for a catering client who wanted to serve cocktails in cupcake form at her garden party. Brilliant woman, fabulous party, very happy guests!

Margarita Lime Zingers

To make the lime curd: Pour 2 inches of water into a small saucepan and top with a shallow stainless steel bowl; it should fit securely in the pan without touching the water. Bring to a boil over high heat. In the top of the double boiler, whisk together the egg yolks, sugar, and lime juice. Continue to whisk constantly until the sugar dissolves and the mixture thickens enough to coat the back of a spoon, 5 to 10 minutes. Remove from the heat and add the butter, two pieces at a time, whisking to melt before adding the next two pieces of butter.

Pour the lime curd into a clean bowl and stir in the tequila. Taste and add more tequila, if desired. Cover with plastic wrap, pressing the plastic directly onto the surface of the curd. Refrigerate until completely chilled and thickened, about 1 hour. The curd can be refrigerated in an airtight container up to 2 weeks.

Preheat the oven to 350°F. Line a 24-cup cupcake pan (or two 12-cup cupcake pans) with cupcake liners.

To make the cupcakes: In a medium bowl, whisk together the flour blend, baking powder, xanthan gum, lime zest, and salt. In a small bowl, combine the milk, lime juice, and tequila. Set both bowls aside.

In the bowl of a stand mixer with the paddle attachment, beat the butter and sugar on medium speed for 2 minutes, or until light and fluffy. Scrape down the bowl. While beating on low, slowly add the egg whites. When all the whites have been added, increase the speed to medium and beat for 30 seconds. Scrape down the bowl.

Add one-fourth of the flour mixture to the butter mixture and mix on low until almost fully incorporated. Add one-third of the milk mixture and beat on low until almost fully incorporated. Repeat with the remaining flour and milk mixtures, starting and ending with the flour. When all the ingredients have been added, scrape down the bowl and beat on medium for 15 seconds.

Pour the batter into the prepared cupcake pans, filling them about three-fourths full. Bake in the center of the oven for about 20 minutes, until the tops are light golden and a toothpick inserted into the center of a cupcake tests clean. Let the cupcakes cool completely on a wire rack.

While the cupcakes bake and cool, make the buttercream: Beat the butter in the bowl of a stand mixer on high speed for 1 minute or until well whipped. Add the confectioners' sugar, cover most of your bowl with a kitchen towel to avoid a dust storm, and beat on low 1 minute to combine. Add the lime juice and zest; beat on low to combine, and then beat on medium for 30 seconds or until well whipped and smooth. You can refrigerate the buttercream in an airtight container for 5 days or freeze for 1 month. Bring to room temperature and beat in the bowl of a stand mixture to restore proper texture before using.

To make the candied zest: Grate about 1 teaspoon of the peel from the lime. In a small saucepan, combine the zest with $\frac{1}{4}$ cup of the cold water. Bring to a simmer; cook for about 5 minutes or until tender, and then drain. Return the zest to the saucepan, stir in the sugar and the remaining $\frac{1}{4}$ cup cold water, and bring to a simmer. Cook on low heat, stirring frequently, until a syrup forms and the zest has become translucent, 10 to 15 minutes. Using a slotted spoon, transfer the zest to a parchment-lined baking sheet to cool completely. The zest can be made up to 1 week ahead and kept at room temperature in an airtight container.

When you're ready to assemble the cupcakes, remove the center of each cupcake, referring to page 174 for guidance. Fill each hole with 1 to 2 tablespoons lime curd (a spoon will do the job), and then ice the tops of the cupcakes with buttercream, referring to page 174 for guidance, if necessary. Just before serving, garnish the cupcakes with the candied lime zest.

TIP

Not all tequilas are gluten free, so be sure to check yours before using. The higher-quality tequilas, like Patrón, are made from 100 percent agave and are therefore naturally gluten free. Look for "100 percent agave" on the label or confirm with the manufacturer that your tequila contains no gluten.

LIME BUTTERCREAM

1 cup (2 sticks) unsalted butter or nonhydrogenated vegetable shortening, at room temperature

3 cups confectioners' sugar (to make your own, see page 192)

1 tablespoon freshly squeezed lime juice

2 teaspoons organic lime zest (optional)

CANDIED LIME ZEST

1 organic lime

½ cup cold water

½ cup organic cane sugar

4

PLATED SLICES
— & little cakes —

Want to put on the ritz? You've come to the right chapter. Each mini cake or slice is individually plated, so guests get to savor their own little cake, gorgeously presented with a special sauce, garnish, or embellishment. But there's no need to be intimidated: These extravagant-looking desserts aren't difficult to pull off if you prepare at least some of the components in advance. Even a pastry chef wouldn't attempt to make these desserts from start to finish the day of the event!

Detailed instructions will also help you perfect dazzling decorations. Drape a petite cake with a chocolaty frill made from modeling chocolate for Chocolate Raspberry Ruffled Cakelets (page 100), or crown layers of cinnamon spice cakelets, caramelized pears, maple syrup, and whipped cream with an elegant crisp Golden Sugar Halo (page 112). Even master a whimsical checkerboard cake composed of strips of rich chocolate cake and even richer White Chocolate Mousse (page 119). And for nostalgia's sake (and because you get to toast the tops of both with the help of a kitchen torch), craft miniaturized versions of two treats that are irresistible to sweet tooths of all ages: the S'mores Cakes (page 108)—a campfire classic ready for a dinner party—and the Baked Alaska Bombes (page 103)—little ice cream cakes iced with meringue. Plan ahead, make components in advance, follow the instructions, and you'll have restaurant-worthy results in no time.

Chocolate Ganache (page 162)

Chocolate Modeling Paste
(page 183)

Chocolate Cake batter (page 63)

MINT CRÈME ANGLAISE

5 egg yolks

2 tablespoons organic cane sugar

Pinch of salt

1½ cups milk or canned
unsweetened coconut milk
(shake cans before opening)

1 to 2 teaspoons pure peppermint
extract

2 or 3 (6-ounce) containers fresh
raspberries, depending on size of
berries

Here you're working with all the components of a layered cake, but in a
deconstructed fashion that lends itself to impressive individual plating. Once
you master this type of dessert, you'll be able to create dozens of variations
by varying the components. Switch out the chocolate cake for Very Vanilla,
Cinnamon Spice, or Lemon cake (pages 140, 59, or 38). Or trade the ganache
for White Chocolate Mousse (page 119) or Lemon Curd (page 38). Everything
can be prepared up to two days in advance (including the ruffles), leaving only
the assembly for you to do on serving day. You'll need a rolling pin and possibly
a pizza cutter for this recipe.

Chocolate Raspberry Ruffled Cakelets

Make the chocolate ganache. Refrigerate until completely chilled and thickened,
at least 2 hours and up to 1 day.

Make the chocolate modeling paste, and let it rest in a resealable plastic bag at least
1 hour and up to 1 day.

Preheat the oven to 350°F. Spray a 13 by 18-inch jelly-roll pan with nonstick cooking
spray, line with parchment paper, and spray again. Pour the batter into the prepared
pan and use an offset spatula or the back of a spoon to spread evenly. Bake in the
center of the oven for 15 to 18 minutes, until the cake bounces back when lightly
pressed and a toothpick inserted into the center tests clean. Transfer the pan to a
wire rack to cool completely.

Using a 3-inch-diameter cookie or biscuit cutter, cut 12 rounds from the cooled sheet
cake. Arrange the rounds on a parchment-lined baking sheet, spacing them so they
do not touch. (Reserve the scraps for snacking or combine with fresh fruit and cream
to make a trifle.) Wrap the sheet with plastic wrap and keep at room temperature
until ready to assemble the cakelets. The cake rounds can be made 2 days ahead;
simply refrigerate the wrapped baking sheet. Or you can freeze them up to 2 weeks,
tightly wrapped in a double layer of plastic wrap; remove from the freezer the night
before you intend to assemble the cakes and allow them to thaw on the countertop
before removing the plastic wrap.

To make the crème anglaise: Create an ice-water bath by filling a stainless steel bowl
with ice cubes and cold water; set aside. Create a double boiler by filling a medium
saucepan with 3 inches of water; top with a stainless steel bowl that fits securely
in the pan without the bottom touching the water. Remove the bowl, and bring the
water in the saucepan to a simmer over medium heat. Meanwhile, off the heat, add
the egg yolks, sugar, and salt to the bowl and whisk to combine; set aside.

In another medium saucepan over medium-high heat, bring the milk just to a simmer. Immediately remove the milk from the heat and pour it over the egg yolk mixture, whisking vigorously to combine. Place the bowl over the simmering water and cook, stirring continuously, until the mixture thickens, about 15 minutes. Once the crème anglaise has thickened enough to coat the back of a spoon, remove the bowl from the saucepan and set in the ice-water bath for about 10 minutes, whisking occasionally to help it cool. Whisk in the peppermint extract to taste. Cover the bowl with plastic wrap and refrigerate to cool completely.

To make the modeling-chocolate ruffles, lightly grease a workspace on your counter using nonstick cooking spray or coconut oil. Transfer the modeling paste from the plastic bag to the counter and knead until pliable, 1 to 2 minutes. Using a rolling pin, roll the paste to $\frac{1}{8}$-inch thickness. Using a paring knife or pizza cutter, cut twelve 3-inch squares. Create a ruffle by pleating and pinching one side of each square with your fingers and easing the opposite side into a gentle fanned-out ruffle shape. Square the pinched end with your knife. Repeat with the remaining squares. Place the ruffles on a parchment-lined baking sheet and set aside until ready to use. The ruffles can be kept at cool room temperature up to 5 days.

To assemble and plate the cakelets, gather together the cake rounds, the ganache, the fresh raspberries, and the modeling-paste ruffles. Scoop or pipe $\frac{1}{4}$ cup ganache onto each cake round and top with a cluster of fresh raspberries. Place one ruffle atop each cakelet, inserting the pinched end through the cluster of berries and down into the ganache to secure it. Adjust the position of the berries to help hold the ruffle in place. Keep the cakelets at room temperature until ready to serve, up to 1 hour.

To avoid sogginess, plate the cakelets no longer than 15 minutes prior to serving. Pour a shallow pool of crème anglaise onto each serving plate. Place one cakelet next to or on top of the crème anglaise. Garnish the plate with additional fresh raspberries.

VARIATION: Vegan Chocolate Raspberry Ruffled Cakelets

Replace the Mint Crème Anglaise with vegan coconut mint whipped "cream": Make Vegan Coconut Whipped Cream (page 117), but add 1 teaspoon pure peppermint extract along with the confectioners' sugar. To plate, transfer the raspberry-topped ruffled cakelets to serving plates and place a dollop of whipped cream alongside.

A baked Alaska is a fun dessert that consists of a layer of cake (I used chocolate, but you could pick any cake batter from chapter 2) topped with a thick slab of ice cream (or sorbet, or gelato, or dairy-free ice cream—it's up to you), blanketed in meringue, and then baked until golden brown. The meringue insulates the ice cream, magically keeping it from melting. Here, I present this dessert baked in individual servings. Don't be deterred by the lengthy instructions—these mini cakes are not difficult to execute, and they can be made well in advance of your party, leaving only the torching of the meringue to do at the last minute.

Baked Alaska Bombes

Preheat the oven to 350°F. Spray a 13 by 18-inch jelly-roll pan with nonstick cooking spray, line with parchment paper, and spray again.

Pour the batter into the prepared pan, and using an offset spatula or the back of a spoon, evenly spread the batter. Bake in the center of the oven for 15 to 18 minutes, until the cake springs back when lightly pressed and a toothpick inserted into the center tests clean. Transfer the pan to a wire rack and let the cake cool completely.

Using a 3-inch-diameter cookie or biscuit cutter, cut 12 rounds from the cooled sheet cake. Arrange the rounds on a parchment-lined baking sheet, spacing them so they do not touch. Wrap the pan of cake rounds with plastic wrap and keep at room temperature until ready to assemble the cakes. Alternatively, you may prepare the cake rounds up to 2 weeks in advance, wrap tightly in plastic wrap, and freeze. Remove from the freezer the night before you intend to assemble the cakes and allow them to thaw on the countertop. (Reserve the scraps for snacking, or combine with fresh fruit and whipped cream to make a trifle.)

Using a 2-ounce ice cream scoop, create 12 well-shaped scoops: press firmly to completely fill the scoop, and then scrape the scoop against the edge of the carton to create flat-bottomed domes. Place one scoop, flat side down, on each cake round.

Immediately place the baking sheet in the freezer for at least 1 hour or until the ice cream is frozen. The bombes can be made to this point up to 1 week in advance; tightly wrap the baking sheet with plastic wrap once the ice cream has frozen solid. While the cake and ice cream are in the freezer, make the puree and meringue.

continued >>

MAKES 12 MINI CAKES (12 SERVINGS)

Chocolate Cake batter
(page 63)

2 pints chocolate hazelnut ice cream, sorbet, gelato, or dairy-free ice cream, or any flavor you prefer

VERY BERRY PUREE

2 cups sliced fresh strawberries

2 cups frozen strawberries (no sugar added)

¼ cup organic cane sugar

1 tablespoon water

2 tablespoons natural strawberry jam

Swiss Meringue Icing (page 165)

Baked Alaska Bombes,
continued >>

To make the puree: Combine the fresh and frozen strawberries, sugar, and water in a medium saucepan over medium heat. Bring to a simmer and cook, stirring occasionally with a wooden spoon, about 15 minutes, until the sugar melts to form a thick syrup with the fruit juices and the berries have become soft enough to mash easily with the spoon. Transfer the berry mixture to a shallow dish to cool for about 15 minutes, and then pour into a blender and blend until smooth. Add the jam and blend again. Place the blender pitcher in the refrigerator until the puree has completely cooled, at least 30 minutes. The puree can be made up to 2 days in advance; transfer to an airtight container and refrigerate.

Just before you are ready to assemble the cakes, make the meringue icing. To assemble and plate the cakes, after the ice cream has frozen solid, remove the pan of ice cream–topped cakes from the freezer. Using the back of a spoon, an offset spatula, or a pastry bag fitted with a star tip, completely cover both the ice cream scoops and the cakes with the meringue icing. Freeze the iced cakes until 15 minutes before you're ready to serve them. You can make the cakes to this point up to 1 week in advance; tightly wrap the baking sheet with plastic wrap once the cakes have frozen solid.

Preheat the oven to broil. Remove the cakes from the freezer and place them under the broiler just until the meringue browns, about 30 seconds. Watch closely while in the oven so the meringue icing does not burn. (Don't worry, if the cakes are frozen solid, the meringue should brown long before the ice cream melts.) Alternatively, if you own a kitchen torch, use the torch to lightly brown the icing on each cake (see page 187 for guidance).

Pour a little pool of puree in the center of each serving plate. Place one cake in the center of each pool. Serve immediately.

TIP ───

You may not need twelve bombes, but don't let that stop you from trying your hand at this dessert. You can easily halve the recipe for the cake, berry puree, and icing.

**FLOURLESS CHOCOLATE
TORTE**

1¼ cups dark chocolate chips

¾ cup melted and cooled virgin
coconut oil (see page 193) or
unsalted butter (1½ sticks)

1 cup organic cane sugar

¾ cup natural (nonalkalized)
cocoa powder

4 eggs or Flax Egg Replacer
(page 194), at room temperature

2 teaspoons pure vanilla extract

CHERRY-BERRY PUREE

2 cups sliced fresh strawberries

1 cup frozen strawberries
(no sugar added)

½ cup frozen cherries
(no sugar added)

3 tablespoons organic cane sugar

1 tablespoon water

It's hard to find an elegant restaurant these days that does not offer a flourless (or nearly flourless) chocolate cake on the dessert menu. But there's no need to make reservations, because this swanky, plated dessert is simple enough to make at home anytime you want to put on the ritz. You'll see that I list coconut oil before butter in this recipe. Butter will work just fine, but I actually prefer the rich flavor of the coconut oil. The sweet-tart puree is the perfect complement to the dense and decadent cake. You can complete the entire cake and accompaniments the day before your party, leaving only the plating to do.

Flourless Chocolate Torte
with Cherry-Berry Puree

To make the cake: Preheat the oven to 300°F. Grease an 8-inch-diameter cake pan with nonstick cooking spray or coconut oil.

Pour 2 inches of water into a small saucepan topped with a shallow stainless steel bowl; it should fit securely in the pan without touching the water. Bring the water to a simmer over medium heat. Place the chocolate chips and coconut oil in the bowl and stir gently over the simmering water until the chocolate has melted. Remove from the heat and whisk until smooth.

Allow the melted chocolate to cool for about 5 minutes, and then whisk in the sugar and cocoa powder until smooth and well combined. Add the eggs and vanilla and whisk just until fully incorporated; don't overbeat the batter.

Pour the batter into the prepared pan and bake for 40 to 50 minutes, until the edges of the cake are dry and the center is set to the touch. The edges may puff up slightly at the end of baking, but the cake will settle as it cools. (Do not use a toothpick test to determine doneness; the cake will still be slightly wet when it has finished baking.) Transfer the pan to a wire rack to cool completely, and then chill in the refrigerator at least 30 minutes before slicing. The cake can be made in advance: tightly wrap the pan in plastic wrap and refrigerate up to 2 days. Or freeze it, wrapped in a double layer of plastic up to 1 month; thaw at least 6 hours on the countertop before unwrapping and serving.

While the cake bakes and cools, make the puree: In a medium saucepan over medium heat, combine the fresh and frozen strawberries, frozen cherries, sugar, and water. Bring the berry mixture to a simmer over medium heat and cook, stirring occasionally with a wooden spoon, about 15 minutes or until the sugar melts to form a thick syrup with the fruit juices and the berries have become soft enough to mash easily with the spoon. Transfer the berry mixture to a shallow dish to cool about 15 minutes, and then pour into a blender and blend until smooth. Place the blender pitcher in the refrigerator until the berry puree has completely cooled, about 30 minutes. The puree can be made up to 2 days in advance; transfer to an airtight container and refrigerate.

When the cake is well chilled, invert the cake pan onto a cutting board, and then flip again so the cake is right-side up. Slice the cake into 12 to 14 slices, depending on the serving size you desire, and let the cake come to room temperature (see Tip). Pour a small pool of berry puree onto each serving plate and, using a cake knife or offset spatula, carefully place a slice of cake next to the pool or directly in it. Serve immediately.

TIP

This cake slices most easily when cold, but should be served at room temperature for the best flavor. Use a warm, dry knife for the cleanest slices. Between each cut, run the knife under hot tap water and wipe dry.

GRAHAM CRACKER BATTER

1 cup (2 sticks) unsalted butter
or Earth Balance Vegan Buttery
Sticks, at room temperature

1½ cups organic cane sugar

2 eggs or Flax Egg Replacer
(page 194)

2 teaspoons pure vanilla extract

2⅔ cups Gluten-Free Whole
Grain Flour Blend (page 191)

1½ cups gluten-free graham
cracker crumbs (I use
Kinnikinnick brand)

2 teaspoons baking powder

2 teaspoons xanthan gum

½ teaspoon fine sea salt

MARSHMALLOW CRÈME

1 cup organic cane sugar

½ cup plus 2 tablespoons light
corn syrup, brown rice syrup,
or honey

⅓ cup water

¼ teaspoon fine sea salt

3 egg whites, at room
temperature

¼ teaspoon cream of tartar

2 teaspoons pure vanilla extract

2 cups dark or semisweet
chocolate chips

12 large natural marshmallows
(see Tip, page 110)

Warning—highly addictive! These sweet riffs on the campfire favorite are more bar than cake, but seriously, are we going to argue about something as scrumptious and nostalgic as a S'mores Cake? I think not. The toasted marshmallows really take these little cakes over the top. You need a kitchen torch or broiler to do the job, but the aroma is sure to conjure up your fondest campfire memories. My recipe for marshmallow crème is not difficult to execute, but a candy thermometer will be essential to your success. Feel free to substitute 10 ounces of your favorite store-bought marshmallow crème. Natural marshmallow crème and natural and even vegan marshmallows are now available in many grocery stores, health foods stores, or online.

S'mores Cakes

To make the batter: In the bowl of a stand mixer with the paddle attachment, beat the butter and sugar on medium speed until light and fluffy, about 3 minutes. Add the eggs and vanilla and beat on medium for 30 seconds. Add the flour blend, graham cracker crumbs, baking powder, xanthan gum, and salt. Mix on low for 15 seconds to combine, and then on medium for 30 seconds to create a thick batter. Set aside. The batter can be prepared up to 2 days in advance; refrigerate in an airtight container.

To make the marshmallow crème: In a small saucepan over high heat, combine the sugar, corn syrup, water, and salt. Bring to a boil, stirring occasionally, until a candy thermometer reads 240°F, about 15 minutes.

Meanwhile, in the bowl of a stand mixer fitted with the whip attachment, beat the egg whites and cream of tartar on medium speed until soft peaks form. You want the egg whites to be ready at the same time as the syrup: if your whites are starting to form peaks before the syrup reaches 240°F, lower the speed on the mixer or stop mixing until the syrup reaches the right temperature. With the mixer on low speed, drizzle in 3 tablespoons of the hot sugar syrup to temper the whites. Continue beating for about 30 seconds.

Drizzle the remaining hot syrup into the egg white mixture, and increase the speed to medium-high, beating until the marshmallow crème is very glossy and stiff, 6 to 8 minutes. Add the vanilla and continue beating for 1 minute. The crème can be made up to 1 week ahead and refrigerated in an airtight container. Bring it to room temperature before using; this will make it easier to spread.

continued >>

Preheat the oven to 350°F and lightly oil a 9 by 13-inch cake pan with nonstick cooking spray or coconut oil. Assemble and bake the cake: Gather together the batter, chocolate chips, and marshmallow crème. Reserve one-third of the batter. Add the remaining two-thirds to the prepared pan, using an offset spatula or the back of a spoon to cover the bottom of the pan evenly.

Scatter the chocolate chips over the batter to cover the top almost completely. Drop large spoonfuls of the marshmallow crème onto the chocolate-chip layer, and use an offset spatula or the back of a spoon to spread the crème evenly. Scatter the reserved batter by tablespoonfuls onto the marshmallow layer in a random fashion, pressing down lightly on the batter to flatten slightly. You will not cover the marshmallow layer completely; there should be some show-through.

Bake for 14 minutes or until the batter is set and just beginning to brown lightly and the marshmallow crème has formed a skin. Do not overbake! You want this cake to be gooey. Transfer the cake in the pan to a wire rack to cool completely. If you cut the cake while it's still warm, you'll have a mess. The cake can be made up to 2 days in advance; wrap the pan tightly with plastic wrap and store at room temperature.

When ready to serve, cut the cake lengthwise into 3 strips, and then cut each strip crosswise into 4 pieces. Transfer to plates and top each serving with one large marshmallow. Using a kitchen torch, lightly brown and melt the marshmallows (see page 187 for guidance). Alternatively, preheat the broiler, place the marshmallows on a baking sheet, and brown for 30 to 60 seconds. Place one toasted marshmallow on each piece of cake and serve immediately.

TIP

Conventional marshmallows are loaded with questionable ingredients, including artificial flavors and colors and genetically modified corn. A natural brand such as Dandies marshmallows (which are also vegan) makes a far better choice. Buy Dandies online at Amazon or at Whole Foods.

There's nothing more decadent than warm molten chocolate cakes served straight from the oven, with the centers still hot and gooey. No adornments, sauces, or garnishes are necessary: this is indulgence in its purest form. The ultra-rich batter comes together in a flash and can be prepared well in advance of a dinner party. When your guests have finished the main course, just pop the cakes in the oven to bake while you clear the dishes and brew some coffee. In only nine minutes, you'll be serving them the most sublime dessert imaginable.

Molten Chocolate Truffle Cakes

MAKES 8 MINI CAKES (8 SERVINGS)

Preheat the oven to 425°F. Lightly oil eight 6-ounce ramekins with butter or coconut oil and dust lightly with cocoa powder. Place the ramekins on a baking sheet and set aside.

Fill a small saucepan with 2 inches of water topped with a stainless steel bowl that fits securely in the pan without the bottom touching the water (you want indirect heat). Place the double boiler over medium heat and add the butter and dark chocolate to the bowl. When the water begins to simmer, reduce the heat to maintain a low simmer until the chocolate and butter have completely melted. Stir or whisk occasionally but do not overwork the chocolate. When the chocolate-butter mixture has melted, turn off the heat and whisk until well combined and smooth.

While the chocolate and butter melt, in the bowl of a stand mixer fitted with the whip attachment, combine the eggs, egg yolks, sugar, and salt. Beat on high speed until the egg mixture is pale and thick, about 6 minutes.

Slowly pour the melted chocolate mixture into the egg mixture and gently fold it in using a rubber spatula. Add the flour and fold it in just to combine.

Gently pour or scoop the batter into the prepared ramekins. Bake for 9 minutes or until the edges and top of the cakes are crusted but the centers are still moist. Transfer the ramekins to a wire rack and let the cakes cool for just 1 minute. Place a serving plate over the top of one ramekin and invert the plate, releasing the cake. Repeat to plate all the cakes. Serve immediately.

1 cup (2 sticks) unsalted butter or melted and cooled virgin coconut oil (see page 193)

Natural (nonalkalized) cocoa powder, for dusting

2½ cups dark chocolate chips

4 eggs, at room temperature

4 egg yolks, at room temperature

½ cup organic cane sugar

Pinch of sea salt

¼ cup Gluten-Free Whole Grain Flour Blend (page 191)

TIP

To make the batter in advance, pour the batter into the greased ramekins, wrap tightly with plastic wrap, and refrigerate for 2 days or freeze up to 1 week. Move from the freezer to your fridge the night before the party, and then to the countertop 2 hours before baking. Keep the ramekins wrapped until you're ready to bake.

Cinnamon Spice Cake batter
(page 59)

GOLDEN SUGAR HALOS

½ cup organic cane sugar

2 tablespoons freshly squeezed
lemon juice

CARAMELIZED PEARS

4 ripe but firm pears (Bartletts
work well), peeled, cored, and
sliced

3 tablespoons freshly squeezed
lemon juice

1 tablespoon plus 1 teaspoon pure
vanilla extract

4 tablespoons unsalted butter or
melted and cooled virgin coconut
oil (see page 193)

1 cup organic cane sugar

MAPLE WHIPPED CREAM

1½ cups ice-cold heavy cream
or canned coconut cream
(refrigerate cans of unsweetened
coconut milk overnight, and then
scoop off the cream)

¼ cup plus 2 tablespoons
maple syrup

Students in my cooking classes invariably start the class believing this recipe (shown on page 115) is beyond their skill level and end the class amazed by their success. The components are no more difficult than any other cake if you break down the steps. Even the sugar halos are deceptively simple to make: just use caution when working with the hot sugar and keep your kids out of the kitchen for that part. And if drizzling the cooked sugar in halo shapes is giving you trouble, just drizzle any simple shape you like, such as a coin or zigzag. It's best to bake this cake the day before you assemble the desserts. The cake will be less fragile to work with after it has settled overnight. Unless it's very humid, it's also a good idea to make the halos the day before to save yourself some time on the day you assemble. Just leave them uncovered overnight.

Cinnamon Mini Cakes with
Caramelized Pears and Golden Sugar Halos

Preheat the oven to 350°F. Spray a 13 by 18-inch jelly-roll pan with nonstick cooking spray, line with parchment paper, and spray again.

Pour the batter into the prepared pan and, using an offset spatula or the back of a spoon, evenly spread out the batter. Bake in the center of the oven for 15 to 18 minutes, until the top is light golden and a toothpick inserted into the center tests clean. Transfer the pan to a wire rack to cool completely.

Using a 3-inch-diameter cookie or biscuit cutter, cut 12 rounds from the cooled sheet cake. Arrange the rounds on a parchment-lined baking sheet, spacing them so they do not touch. (Reserve the scraps for snacking or to combine with fresh fruit and cream to make a trifle.) Tightly wrap the pan with plastic wrap and keep at room temperature up to 2 days or until ready to assemble cakes.

To make the sugar halos: Line a heavy baking sheet with parchment paper; set aside. In a heavy-bottomed medium saucepan over medium heat, combine the sugar and lemon juice, stirring to moisten the sugar with the juice. Allow the sugar to melt, swirling the pan slowly for even melting. Bring the sugar mixture to a boil and continue boiling for 3 minutes.

Immediately remove from the heat and let cool for 2 minutes. Working quickly and carefully, hold the saucepan over the prepared sheet and dip a metal spoon into the sugar syrup (wrap the handle of the spoon with a kitchen towel if it gets hot); drizzle the sugar in circular halo shapes onto the parchment (see page 114). Do not touch the sugar syrup—it will burn you! If necessary, use the spoon to trace the halo pattern through the sugar to make sure your halos form complete circles. This will ensure that they hold their shape on the finished cakes.

You will have more sugar halos than you need to top the 6 cakes, but that's okay as some may break. (Any leftover halos can be crushed into "golden sugar" bits and scattered decoratively around the serving plates.) Allow the halos to cool completely before touching them, at least 15 minutes. In dry weather, you can make the halos 3 days in advance; if it's humid, make them the day you intend to use them. Set aside.

Make the caramelized pears the day you plan to serve the cakes: Preheat the oven to 375°F. In a medium bowl, toss the pear slices with the lemon juice and vanilla to coat well. Melt the butter in a large ovenproof skillet over medium-high heat. Add the sugar and shake the pan to moisten the sugar with the butter. Add the pear slices and all the liquid from the bowl and cook until the sugar dissolves and the mixture bubbles, about 3 minutes, shaking the pan frequently to keep the pears from sticking. Place the skillet in the oven and bake until the pears are soft and the juices are lightly browned, about 10 minutes. Carefully remove the pan from the oven and pour the pears and caramelized syrup into a medium bowl. Set aside at room temperature until ready to assemble the cakes.

While the pears bake, make the whipped cream: In a stand mixer with the whisk attachment, beat the cream on high until soft peaks form, about 5 minutes. Add the maple syrup and continue beating until the cream forms firm peaks. Refrigerate until ready to use, up to 3 hours. If you keep it longer, the cream may separate and become weepy. (If it does, beat again before using.)

To assemble and plate the cakes, gather together the cake rounds (two per cake), caramelized pears (make sure they are completely cool—if they're warm, the hot caramel will make the stacked cakes slide around), chilled whipped cream, and cooled sugar halos.

Place one round of cake on a serving plate and top with some of the pears and caramel. Add a dollop of whipped cream and then another round of cake, pressing down gently. Finish with more whipped cream and a sugar halo nestled into the cream. If you have extra caramelized pears, you can spoon them around the cake in a decorative fashion. Extra golden sugar bits can be sprinkled on the pears or around the edge of the plate. Repeat with the remaining cakes, pears, and whipped cream. Serve immediately.

TIP

You can assemble the cakes up to 1 hour in advance and keep at cool room temperature until serving time. But wait to place the halos in the cream until just before serving or they will become soft. Do not refrigerate the sugar halos at any point in the process, as they will become soft and "weepy" with condensation.

Golden Sugar Halos technique and Cinnamon Mini Cakes (page 112)

Chocolate Cake batter
(page 63)

Chocolate Ganache (page 162)

**GRAND MARNIER CRÈME
ANGLAISE**

5 large egg yolks

2 tablespoons organic cane sugar

Pinch of salt

1½ cups milk or canned
unsweetened coconut milk
(shake cans before opening)

1 vanilla bean pod, halved
lengthwise and seeds reserved, or
1 teaspoon pure vanilla extract

2 to 4 teaspoons Grand Marnier

1 tablespoon freshly squeezed
orange juice

2 oranges, peeled and sectioned,
for garnish

This is an impressive-looking dessert that may appear to be too complicated for the home baker, but nothing could be further from the truth. The various components—cake, ganache, and crème anglaise (a rich custard sauce)—are simple enough and all can be prepared in advance. Extra crème anglaise is wonderful drizzled over fresh fruit or as an accompaniment to almost any dessert.

Chocolate Orange Gâteaux
with Grand Marnier Crème Anglaise

Preheat the oven to 350°F. Spray a 13 by 18-inch jelly-roll pan with nonstick cooking spray, line with parchment paper, and spray again. To make the cake, pour the batter into the prepared pan and evenly spread out the batter. Bake in the center of the oven for 15 to 18 minutes, until a toothpick inserted into the center tests clean. Transfer the pan to a wire rack to cool completely.

Using a 3-inch-diameter cookie or biscuit cutter, cut 12 rounds from the cooled sheet cake. Arrange the rounds on a parchment-lined baking sheet, spacing them so they do not touch. Wrap the pan of cake rounds with plastic wrap and keep at room temperature until ready to assemble the cakes. (Alternatively, you can prepare the cake rounds up to 2 weeks in advance, wrap tightly in plastic wrap, and freeze. Remove from the freezer the night before you intend to assemble the cakes and allow them to thaw on the countertop.) Place the cake scraps in the bowl of a food processor and pulse until you have fine crumbs. Cover the crumbs and reserve or freeze them in a resealable plastic bag up to 2 weeks.

While the cakes bake and cool, prepare the ganache. Divide between 2 bowls and tightly cover with plastic wrap. Place half in the refrigerator to firm up for at least 45 minutes and keep half at room temperature. You will use half to fill the gâteaux and the other half for glazing.

While the ganache chills, make the crème anglaise: Create an ice-water bath by filling a stainless steel bowl with ice cubes and cold water; set aside. Create a double boiler by filling a medium saucepan with 3 inches of water topped with a stainless steel bowl that fits securely into the pan without the bottom touching the water (you want indirect heat). Remove the bowl, and bring the water in the saucepan to a simmer over medium heat. Meanwhile, off the heat, add the egg yolks, sugar, and salt to the bowl and whisk to combine; set aside.

In another medium saucepan over medium-high heat, combine the milk and vanilla-bean seeds and bring just to a simmer (if using vanilla extract, don't add it yet). Immediately remove the milk from the heat and pour it over the egg yolk mixture, whisking vigorously to combine. Place the bowl over the simmering water and cook, stirring continuously, until the custard thickens, about 15 minutes.

Once the crème anglaise has thickened enough to coat the back of a spoon, remove the bowl from the saucepan and set in the ice-water bath for about 10 minutes, whisking occasionally to help cool it. Whisk in the Grand Marnier to taste, and then add the orange juice (and vanilla extract, if using), whisking to combine. Cover the bowl with plastic wrap and refrigerate to cool completely.

To assemble and plate the cakes, gather together the cake rounds, the ganache, the crème anglaise, and the oranges. Half of your ganache should be cool and thick enough to use as a filling, while the other half should be pourable for glazing. If necessary, you can rewarm the ganache for glazing in the microwave until it reaches a pourable consistency.

You will use three rounds of cake for each gâteau. Place one cake round on your work surface. Spoon about 2 tablespoons of the chilled ganache filling onto the cake and use the back of the spoon to spread it to the edges of the cake. Add the second cake round and press it firmly into the ganache. Repeat the ganache application and then top with the third round of cake. Repeat until you have four gâteaux.

Using a spatula, transfer your stacked gâteaux to a wire rack placed over a baking sheet. Pour $\frac{1}{3}$ cup of the room-temperature glaze over each gâteau, allowing excess ganache to spill over the edges of the cakes. Focus on making the tops of the gâteaux attractive; use an offset spatula or the back of a spoon to smooth the tops and make sure they are evenly coated. When the glaze has stopped dripping down the sides of the cakes, use an offset spatula or butter knife to smooth the sides, but don't fuss if they aren't perfectly smooth. Allow the gâteaux to sit until the ganache is set but still tacky, about 15 minutes.

Pick up a handful of crumbs and press them onto the sides of each cake, creating a velvet or sueded appearance. You can prepare the gâteaux to this point up to 1 day ahead; transfer the cakes to a baking sheet, tent with plastic wrap, and refrigerate. Bring to room temperature before serving.

When you're ready to serve, carefully transfer the gâteaux onto serving plates using a spatula. Pour the crème anglaise around each cake. Place 2 or 3 orange segments on top of each cake and scatter the remaining segments in the crème anglaise. Serve immediately.

VARIATION: Chocolate Orange Gâteaux with Vegan Coconut Whipped Cream

To make a vegan version of this cake, replace the crème anglaise with Vegan Coconut Whipped Cream: In a stand mixer with the whip attachment, beat 1½ cups ice-cold canned coconut cream (refrigerate cans of coconut milk overnight, and then scoop off the cream) until soft peaks form, about 5 minutes. Add 1 tablespoon confectioners' sugar and continue to beat until the cream forms firm peaks. Refrigerate until ready to use, up to 6 hours. To plate, follow the instructions above.

Your guests will believe you are a master in the kitchen when you present this dramatic dessert. Not only does the cake look like it was created by a magician, but it also features a striking combo of white and dark chocolate. Just follow my step-by-step instructions to create the checkerboard pattern. I leave the option of covering the cake with chocolate or white chocolate ganache up to you; they're both exquisite. Like any multicomponent dessert, preparing at least some elements in advance is key. Any leftover mousse can be refrigerated in an airtight container up to 1 week. Serve with fresh fruit or use as a filling between two cookies to create a sandwich cookie.

White and Dark Chocolate Checkerboard Cake

Preheat the oven to 350°F. Spray a 13 by 18-inch jelly-roll pan with nonstick cooking spray, line with parchment paper, and spray again.

Pour the batter into the prepared pan and use an offset spatula or the back of a spoon to spread evenly. Bake in the center of the oven for 15 to 18 minutes, until the cake bounces back when lightly pressed in the center and a toothpick inserted into the center tests clean. Transfer the cake to a wire rack to cool completely. While the cake bakes and cools, make the mousse and ganache.

To make the mousse: Create a double boiler by filling a small saucepan with 1 inch of water topped with a stainless steel bowl that fits securely in the pan without the bottom touching the water. Bring the water to a low simmer over medium heat; do not boil. Place the white chocolate chips in the top of the double boiler and melt slowly, occasionally stirring the chocolate gently with a rubber spatula; do not overwork the chocolate. If the water starts to boil rapidly, remove the double boiler from the heat or reduce the heat level so the water returns to a simmer.

Meanwhile, in the bowl of a stand mixer with a whisk attachment, combine the cream, egg whites, and vanilla and beat on medium-high speed until soft peaks form. When the chocolate has completely melted, remove the bowl from the double boiler, wipe the bottom of the bowl dry, and allow to cool slightly, about 5 minutes. Add one-third of the whipped cream mixture to the melted white chocolate and stir vigorously until completely incorporated and smooth. Add the remaining whipped cream and, using a rubber spatula, gently fold together. Keep the mousse at room temperature up to 1 hour, until ready to assemble the cake. Or you can make it up to 2 days in advance; refrigerate in an airtight container and bring to room temperature before assembling the cake.

continued >>

MAKES ONE 9 BY 5-INCH LOAF
(8 TO 10 SERVINGS)

Chocolate Cake batter (page 63)

WHITE CHOCOLATE MOUSSE

4 cups white chocolate chips

2½ cups heavy cream

2 egg whites, at room temperature

2 teaspoons pure vanilla extract

Chocolate Ganache (page 162) or White Chocolate Ganache (page 163)

Next, make the ganache. You can refrigerate it in an airtight container for up to 1 week. Bring to room temperature before glazing the cake.

To assemble and plate the cake, gather together the cake, mousse, and a 9 by 5-inch loaf pan. Lightly oil the pan with nonstick cooking spray or coconut oil and line with plastic wrap, covering the bottom and sides completely and leaving extra wrap hanging over the sides (the extra will be used as handles to remove the checkerboard cake). Use multiple pieces of plastic wrap if necessary.

Cut the sheet cake into 1-inch-wide strips, and then cut the strips into 9-inch-long pieces. The length is determined by the length of the loaf pan; you can set the loaf pan gently atop the cake strips and mark the length to be cut. (You will have more strips than you need.)

Arrange 2 strips in the bottom of the loaf pan, one along each side. Clean up any crumbs that fall in the open spaces or channels between the strips of cake. The channels will be narrower than the cake strips.

Place the mousse in a piping bag fitted with a large round tip. Alternatively, you may use a large resealable plastic bag with one corner snipped. Pipe the mousse into the channel between the cake strips, filling the spaces completely. Tap the pan gently on the counter to settle the mousse, and pipe more mousse if necessary to fill. Gently lay 1 cake strip atop the channel of mousse. Pipe mousse in the space between the cake strips (this will be on top of the first layer of cake strips), gently tapping the pan on the counter again to settle the mousse and adding more if necessary. Lay 2 cake strips atop the second layer of mousse and pipe mousse to fill in the open channel. Congratulations, you have completed the checkerboard pattern! Gently fold the overhanging plastic wrap over the cake and mousse, adding another piece of plastic, if necessary, to cover the cake completely. Refrigerate until the cake and mousse are firm, at least 2 hours and up to 1 day. (You can tightly wrap the cooled loaf in its pan in a double layer of plastic wrap and freeze up to 2 weeks. Move the loaf pan to the refrigerator the day before you plan to proceed with glazing.)

Line a baking sheet with parchment paper and place a wire rack over the pan. Remove the chilled cake from the refrigerator and unwrap the plastic covering the top of the cake. To release the cake, gently invert the pan onto the rack and remove the remaining plastic wrap. Pour the ganache over the cake and, using an offset spatula or butter knife, evenly spread the glaze, allowing it to drip down to completely cover the sides of the cake. Allow the glaze to set. Using a spatula and your hand to steady the cake, gently transfer the cake to a cutting board (or simply leave it on the wire rack) and refrigerate at least 30 minutes and up to 1 day.

The cake will be easiest to slice when cold, but you'll want to serve it at room temperature for the fullest flavor. Cut the chilled cake into 8 to 10 even slices, but don't separate the slices from the loaf until ready to serve. If you want your checkerboards to stand up, cut thicker slices. Thinner slices will lie flat. When you're ready to serve, place a slice of checkerboard cake on each plate.

CAKE

¾ cup plus 3 tablespoons organic cane sugar

¾ cup Gluten-Free Whole Grain Flour Blend (page 191)

1¼ cups egg whites (from about 10 eggs), at room temperature

2 teaspoons pure vanilla extract

1 teaspoon cream of tartar

¼ teaspoon fine sea salt

¾ cup confectioners' sugar, for rolling the cake (to make your own, see page 192)

1½ cups raspberry preserves

Glossy Chocolate Glaze (page 164)

CHAMBORD CRÈME ANGLAISE

5 egg yolks

2 tablespoons organic cane sugar

Pinch of salt

1½ cups milk or canned unsweetened coconut milk (shake cans before opening)

1 vanilla bean pod, halved lengthwise and seeds reserved, or 1 teaspoon pure vanilla extract

2 to 4 teaspoons Chambord (black raspberry liqueur)

1½ cups fresh raspberries, for garnish

Spread raspberry preserves on a vanilla cake made in a jelly-roll pan; roll up the cake and chill before drizzling it with a decadent chocolate glaze. When you're ready to serve, slice the cake to reveal the raspberry swirl, plate the slices on an extravagant Chambord crème anglaise, and garnish with fresh raspberries. Then sit back and watch your guests swoon.

Chocolate-Glazed Raspberry-Vanilla Jelly Roll
with Chambord Crème Anglaise

Preheat the oven to 350°F. Spray a 13 by 18-inch jelly-roll pan with nonstick cooking spray, line the pan with parchment paper, and spray again.

To make the cake: Combine ¾ cup of the cane sugar and the flour blend in a medium bowl; sift the mixture twice. In the bowl of a stand mixer fitted with the whisk attachment, beat together the egg whites, vanilla, cream of tartar, and salt on medium speed until soft peaks form. Gradually beat in the remaining 3 tablespoons cane sugar, 1 tablespoon at a time. Remove the bowl from the mixer and, using the whisk attachment with your hand, blend in the flour mixture in 3 batches.

Gently pour the batter into the prepared pan and, using an offset spatula or the back of a large spoon, smooth out the batter so it's evenly spread to the edges and into the corners of the pan. Bake on the bottom oven rack for 12 to 15 minutes, or until the top is light golden brown and a toothpick inserted into the center tests clean.

While the cake is baking, spread out a tea towel on your counter and sprinkle it with about half of the confectioners' sugar. When the cake has finished baking, immediately turn it out onto the prepared towel. Peel off the parchment and sprinkle the remaining confectioners' sugar to lightly cover the cake. Position the cake so the short edge faces you. Using the short edge of the tea towel, roll up the cake completely, using the towel to guide you and rolling the towel inside the cake (don't worry, we're going to take it out later!). Set aside on a wire rack to cool. While the cake cools, make the glaze. You can refrigerate it in an airtight container for up to 1 week. Bring to room temperature before glazing the cake.

When the cake is completely cool to the touch, carefully unroll it. Spread the preserves evenly over the cake, leaving a 1-inch gap around the edges. Reroll the cake, without the tea towel this time; wrap tightly in plastic wrap and refrigerate at least 1 hour and up to 2 days. You can freeze the rolled cake up to 1 month; freeze unwrapped until solid, and then tightly wrap in two layers of plastic wrap and a single layer of aluminum foil and return to the freezer.

To make the crème anglaise: Create an ice-water bath by filling a stainless steel bowl with ice cubes and cold water; set aside. Create a double boiler by filling a medium saucepan with 3 inches of water topped with a stainless steel bowl that fits securely in the pan without the bottom touching the water (you want indirect heat). Remove the bowl, and bring the water in the saucepan to a simmer over medium heat. Meanwhile, off the heat, add the egg yolks, sugar, and salt to the bowl and whisk to combine; set aside.

In another medium saucepan over medium-high heat, combine the milk and vanilla bean seeds and bring just to a simmer (if using vanilla extract, don't add it yet). Immediately remove the milk from the heat and pour it over the egg yolk mixture, whisking vigorously to combine. Place the bowl over the simmering water and cook, stirring continuously, until the custard thickens, about 15 minutes.

Once the crème anglaise has thickened enough to coat the back of a spoon, remove the bowl from the saucepan and set it in the ice-water bath to cool about 10 minutes, whisking occasionally to help cool it. Whisk in Chambord to taste and vanilla extract, if using. Cover the bowl with plastic wrap and refrigerate to cool completely.

Transfer the chilled cake to a wire rack with a baking sheet underneath to catch any drips. Drizzle the glaze over the cake from side to side to create a zigzag effect, allowing the glaze to run over the sides of the cake. After the glaze sets, you can refrigerate the cake up to 5 days. The cake will taste best served at room temperature, but it's easiest to plate when it's cold.

To ready the cake for plating, using a large spatula and one hand, transfer the chilled cake to a cutting board. Cut the cake into 8 to 10 even slices (to create the cleanest slices, run your knife under warm water after each cut and wipe dry before proceeding), but don't separate the slices until you're ready to serve. If you want the slices to stand up on the plate, cut thicker slices; thinner slices will lie flat. When you're ready to serve, pour a shallow pool of the crème anglaise onto each serving plate. Place a slice of the jelly-roll cake on top, either standing up or lying flat. Garnish the plates with the fresh raspberries.

DECORATED
SPECIAL-
OCCASION
cakes

My passion for making elaborate decorated cakes started simply enough, with a cake for my son's peewee soccer team. We were planning the celebratory end-of-season party and, when the moms divvied up the food assignments, I offered to bring dessert. But in typical type-A fashion, I made an over-the-top cake—a grassy green soccer field topped with a sculpted soccer ball decorated with a blue first-place ribbon and a cluster of handmade roses, plus pennants with each boy's name surrounding the field.

As a pastry chef, my focus had been on plated presentations, so I had never actually created a decorated cake. I'll admit, this cake was an ambitious first attempt. In fact, I spent the better part of a week playing around with fondant, modeling chocolate, and gel colors to design that cake. The other moms were so wowed by my soccer cake that I left the party with birthday cake orders for several of their children. Just like that, my cake biz was born.

You don't need to be a cake artist to make and decorate the cakes in this chapter, or own a lot of fancy tools and equipment (each recipe includes a short list of the tools you'll need)—just the willingness to think big, unleash your creativity, and have some fun. To help ensure impressive results, the recipes take you through every single step, providing lots of tricks and tips learned from my own successes (and mishaps) along the way. Happily, many of the components of these decorated cakes can be made ahead of time, so you don't have to try to do it all on the big day. Be creative, have fun, and don't stress. Just enjoy the process, because even your "mistakes" will be delicious!

Chocolate Modeling Paste
(page 183)

White Chocolate Modeling
Paste (page 183), recipe doubled

Very Vanilla Cake batter
(page 40)

Very Vanilla Buttercream
(page 161), at room temperature

SPECIAL TOOLS

Rolling pin

Pizza wheel or paring knife

Instead of giving your loved ones a gift wrapped in a pretty package, give them a pretty cake that's shaped like a present! The cake is wrapped up in pliable sheets of modeling chocolate, and the ribbons and bow are cut from this delicious material, too. The chocolate paste sheets yield results similar to fondant, but you can easily make them at home with just two ingredients. I love the classic look of a white-chocolate box wrapped with dark chocolate ribbons, but you could also color the white chocolate modeling paste. For tips on wrapping a cake with modeling chocolate and making modeling chocolate decor, see page 183.

Pretty as a Package Cake

Make the chocolate and white chocolate modeling pastes through the kneading step. Place each type of modeling paste in a separate resealable plastic bag and seal the bags. Let rest at cool room temperature at least 1 hour and up to 1 day. If either mixture is very sticky, place it on a piece of parchment paper and allow it to air dry for 30 minutes before placing in the bag to rest.

Preheat the oven to 350°F. Lightly oil a 13 by 18-inch jelly-roll pan with nonstick cooking spray, line it with parchment paper, and spray again. Pour the batter evenly into the pan and bake in the center of the oven for 12 to 15 minutes, until the top is light golden and a toothpick inserted into the center tests clean. Transfer the cake to a wire rack to cool completely.

When the cake has completely cooled, run a knife along the edges of the cake to loosen it from the sides of the pan. Invert the pan over a cutting board or onto your parchment-lined counter. Using a sharp knife, cut away the outside $\frac{1}{2}$-inch of cake around all four edges. Discard this crusty edge.

Using a measuring tape or ruler for guidance, cut six 5-inch squares from the sheet of cake. (You will use only five for the cake, but reserve the sixth in case one of your squares breaks.) Wrap the cake layers tightly in plastic wrap and set aside until ready to assemble the cake. The cake layers can be frozen, tightly wrapped in a double layer of plastic wrap, up to 1 month. Thaw at room temperature before frosting and decorating.

Prepare the buttercream; keep at room temperature until ready to use, or make it ahead and refrigerate in an airtight container for up to 5 days.

To assemble the cake, gather together the cake layers, buttercream, modeling paste, and special tools. If you premade the buttercream and stored it in the refrigerator, bring it to room temperature and beat in the bowl of a stand mixer to restore its texture before proceeding.

continued >>

Pretty as a Package Cake,
continued >>

Place one of the cake layers on a serving platter. Scoop $\frac{1}{4}$ cup buttercream onto the cake and, using an offset spatula or butter knife, spread the frosting to create a thin, even layer that covers the cake all the way to the edges. You may be tempted to use a larger amount of buttercream between the cake layers, but spreading only a thin layer will make the cake much easier to assemble, frost, decorate, and slice. Repeat with the remaining 4 layers, pressing each layer firmly onto the layer below it, but do not spread any buttercream on the top layer. Using the offset spatula or butter knife, wipe away any excess buttercream that extends beyond the edges of the cake layers. Place the cake (no need to cover or wrap) in the refrigerator for 1 hour or so to firm up the buttercream. Cover the remaining buttercream with plastic wrap and let it sit at room temperature.

While the cake chills, make the chocolate bows and ribbons. Lightly grease your countertop with nonstick cooking spray. Remove the dark chocolate modeling paste from the plastic bag, place it on the prepared counter, and knead until the chocolate forms a pliable paste, about 1 minute.

Using a rolling pin, roll the paste to $\frac{1}{8}$-inch thickness. Use a pizza wheel or paring knife to cut four 1-inch-wide ribbons that are 9 inches long; be sure to square off the ends. These will be the ribbons that wrap your cake. Transfer the ribbons to a baking sheet lined with parchment paper and cover with plastic wrap so they stay pliable.

Cut two more ribbons to form the tails of your bow; these should also be 1 inch wide, but only 4 inches long each. Use a paring knife to cut a V-shape notch in one end of each ribbon. Transfer to the baking sheet and re-cover to keep pliable.

To form the bow, cut another ribbon that measures 2 by 7 inches. Lay the ribbon horizontally in front of you. Lift both ends and fold them toward the center until the ends meet. Press the ends down lightly, but do not deflate the loops you have created with the folds. Using your forefinger and thumb, gently pinch the middle of the ribbon between the loops to create your bow. Cut a small rectangle of modeling chocolate, about 1 by 2 inches, and cover the center of your bow, tucking the ends of the rectangle underneath the bow. Set the bow on another baking sheet, but do not cover it with plastic wrap. You can keep the modeling paste bow and tails at cool room temperature up to 3 days, but the ribbons that crisscross the cake should be made the day you decorate so they drape smoothly over the cake.

When the cake is chilled, gather together the cake and reserved room-temperature buttercream. Frost the top and sides of the cake with the buttercream, paying extra attention to the corners and squaring off the edges as much as possible. Refer to page 173 for guidance, if necessary. Return the cake to the refrigerator to chill about 1 hour; the buttercream must be quite firm before you wrap it with the white chocolate sheet and position the chocolate ribbons and bow (see Tip).

When the buttercream is firm, remove the chilled cake from the refrigerator. Roll out the white chocolate modeling paste to $\frac{1}{8}$-inch thickness and immediately use it to cover the cake completely, following the instructions on page 184. Remove the plastic wrap from the decor. Begin with the 1 by 9-inch ribbons that will crisscross your gift box. Use an offset spatula or paring knife to lift up the ribbon, if necessary; working with your hands, position one end of one ribbon where the cake meets the plate. Gently press the ribbon against the cake while lifting it up and over the top of the cake, just as you would wrap a ribbon around a package. If your ribbons do not want to adhere to the cake, use a very slightly dampened fingertip to moisten the bottoms of the ribbons. The top end should be centered on the top of the cake. If you have some extra ribbon, cut it away with your knife. Repeat with the remaining three ribbons so that they crisscross the box, trimming off any excess so the ribbons all meet in the center of the cake.

Slightly wet your finger with water and just barely dampen the area where all of the ribbons meet. Next, you'll add the two 1 by 4-inch bow tails: Working with one tail at a time, affix the squared ends of the tails to the dampened spot at the center of the cake and allow the notched ends to trail over the cake and down the sides. Do not press the tails of the ribbons into the cake; you want them to look loose and flowing. Again, dampen the spot at the center of the cake where the ribbons crisscross, and gently lift and place the bow atop the cake so it covers the tops of the tails.

Keep the decorated cake at cool room temperature until ready to serve, up to 1 day. To make the cake up to 2 days in advance, fill and frost the cake and refrigerate it, uncovered, but reserve the modeling chocolate wrap, ribbons, and bow, applying them the day you plan to serve the cake. Modeling chocolate decor should not be refrigerated as it may suffer from condensation, bleed, or turn soft.

To serve, cut the cake in half through the center, where the ribbons crisscross at the top, and then cut the cake at a right angle to this first cut to make ten 1-inch-thick slices. Transfer to serving plates. The cake will taste best at room temperature.

TIP

If your cake is very cold when you apply the chocolate wrap and decor, you may find that the modeling paste develops tiny beads of condensation. Don't panic and don't touch the condensation or try to wipe it dry. Let it sit and it will dry out on its own.

Chocolate Modeling Paste
(page 183)

White Chocolate Modeling
Paste (page 183), recipe halved

Lemon Cake batter (page 38)

Coconut Buttercream
(page 158)

Natural gel food coloring, your
choice of color, for the heart

SPECIAL TOOLS

Rolling pin

Heart-shaped cookie cutter of
any size

Rotary pizza cutter

Plastic or latex gloves (optional)

Celebrate your special someone with this zebra-stripe cake with a heart at its center. The various components can be prepared well in advance of your celebration, and the entire cake can be completed the day before. You can switch up the lemon batter and coconut buttercream for any flavors you like from the recipes in chapters 2 and 6. For the best effect, you want a light-colored frosting here.

Wild at Heart Cake

Make the chocolate and white chocolate modeling pastes through the kneading step according to the recipe instructions. Place each type of modeling paste in a separate resealable plastic bag and seal the bags. Let rest at cool room temperature at least 1 hour and up to 1 day. If either mixture is very sticky, place it on a piece of parchment paper and allow it to air-dry for 30 minutes before placing in the bag to rest.

Preheat the oven to 350°F. Lightly oil two 8-inch-diameter cake pans with nonstick cooking spray or coconut oil. Pour the batter into the prepared pans and bake as the recipe instructs, using a toothpick to test for doneness. Transfer the cakes to wire racks to cool for 10 minutes or until the cake pans are cool enough to safely handle, and then invert onto the racks to cool completely. You can freeze the cooled cake layers, tightly wrapped in a double layer of plastic wrap, up to 1 month; thaw at room temperature before frosting the cake.

While the cakes bake and cool, make the buttercream, mixing in the coconut extract. Cover the bowl of the buttercream with plastic wrap and set aside at cool room temperature or transfer to an airtight container and refrigerate up to 5 days.

To assemble the cake, gather together the cake layers and buttercream. If you made the buttercream ahead and stored it in the refrigerator, bring it to room temperature and beat in the bowl of a stand mixer to restore its texture before proceeding.

Split each cake layer horizontally in half, referring to page 173 for guidance. Spread ½ cup buttercream between each layer, but do not frost the top of the cake. Using an offset spatula or butter knife, wipe away any buttercream that extends beyond the edges of the layers, and chill your cake until firm, about 1 hour. Cover the remaining buttercream with plastic wrap and set aside at cool room temperature.

While the cake chills, make the modeling chocolate decor. Lightly grease your countertop with nonstick cooking spray. Remove the white modeling chocolate from the plastic bag and knead the paste on the counter until pliable. You will use it to make the heart. Using red gel coloring (or a color of your choice), color the modeling paste. Your hands may become stained, so it's a good idea to wear plastic or latex gloves. Use a toothpick to transfer 1 drop of the gel from the container to the modeling paste, and knead the gel into the paste. It takes only a tiny bit of gel to achieve brilliant color, but if you need more, add another drop. Roll the paste to $\frac{1}{4}$-inch thickness. Using a heart-shaped cookie cutter (any size you have is fine; I use a 4-inch cutter), cut out a heart and transfer it to a parchment-lined baking sheet.

Set aside the sheet with the colored white chocolate heart until ready to proceed with assembly. If preparing more than 6 hours in advance, cover the sheet with plastic wrap and keep at cool room temperature. The heart may be prepared up to 4 days before assembly.

Lightly grease your countertop with nonstick cooking spray. Remove the dark modeling chocolate from the plastic bag and knead the paste on the counter until pliable. You will use this to make the zebra stripes.

Roll out the chocolate modeling paste to $\frac{1}{8}$-inch thickness to form a rectangle approximately 14 by 6 inches. Square off the sides and remove the excess. Using the rotary cutter, cut zebra stripes, pointed at one end and straight at the other, starting at the bottom left corner and zigzagging from bottom to top and back with your cutter. After the whole piece of paste is cut, immediately transfer the stripes to the baking sheet with the heart and cover with plastic wrap to keep them from drying out.

Frost the top and sides of the cake with the remaining buttercream, referring to page 173 for guidance, if necessary. Return the frosted cake to the refrigerator to firm up, about 1 hour. The buttercream needs to be quite firm before you place the modeling chocolate decor on the cake.

When the cake is well chilled, gather together the cake and pan of decorations. Remove one stripe at a time to transfer to the cake, keeping the remaining stripes covered with plastic wrap. Pick up the stripe by the blunt end and grasp the tip with your other hand; align the straight edge of the stripe with the bottom or top edge of the cake and gently smooth the stripe out toward the tip onto the sides of the cake. Alternate the stripes, pointy sides up, then down, working all the way around the sides of the cake tier. A zebra pattern is irregular, so don't stress out about placing the stripes perfectly.

Lift your heart from the tray, using the tip of a knife to help release it from the baking sheet, if necessary, and cradle the heart in one palm to prevent stretching. Center the heart on the top of the cake and lightly press it down with your palm.

Store the finished cake in an airtight container (or tented with plastic wrap) until ready to serve, up to 1 day. The cake will taste best served at room temperature. To make the cake up to 2 days in advance, don't apply the modeling chocolate decor until the day you plan to serve the cake. The decor should not be refrigerated as it may suffer from condensation and bleed or turn soft.

White Chocolate Modeling
Paste (page 183), recipe doubled

Pink Velvet Strawberry Cake
batter (page 52)

PINK BUTTERCREAM

1 cup (2 sticks) unsalted butter
or nonhydrogenated vegetable
shortening, at room temperature

3½ cups confectioners' sugar (to
make your own, see page 192)

2 teaspoons pure vanilla extract
or 1 teaspoon peppermint extract

Pink natural gel food coloring

SPECIAL TOOLS

Rolling pin

Crown-shaped cookie cutter

Plastic or latex gloves (optional)

Children's birthday parties should be a time of great joy and indulgence, but
they can be fraught with stress and frustration when your kiddo is gluten free.
Long before my own son and I began following gluten-free diets, I was making
g-free birthday cakes at my bakery for children who couldn't eat gluten. This
cake features layers of pink inside and out. To make the cake especially regal, it
is baked in three 6-inch pans so it's extra-tall, topped with a crown, and dotted
with dainty pearls made from white chocolate modeling paste.

Pink Princess Cake

Make the white chocolate modeling paste through the kneading step according to the
instructions. Transfer to a resealable plastic bag and seal the bag. Let rest at cool room
temperature at least 1 hour and up to 1 day. If the mixture is very sticky, place it on
a piece of parchment paper and allow it to air-dry for 30 minutes before placing it in
the bag to rest.

While the modeling paste rests, make the cake. Preheat the oven to 350°F. Lightly oil
three 6-inch round cake pans with nonstick cooking spray or coconut oil. Pour the
batter into the prepared pans and bake for about 20 minutes, using a toothpick to test
for doneness. Remove the cakes from the oven and place on wire racks to cool for
10 minutes or until the pans are cool enough to safely handle. Then invert onto the
racks to cool completely. The cake layers can be made ahead: wrap tightly in plastic
wrap and refrigerate up to 2 days. Or wrap in a double layer of plastic and freeze up
to 1 month; thaw at room temperature before removing the plastic.

While the cakes bake and cool, make the buttercream: In the bowl of a stand mixer
with the paddle attachment, beat the butter on high speed for 1 minute until well
whipped. Add the confectioners' sugar and cover most of your bowl with a kitchen
towel; beat on low for 1 minute to combine, and then whip on medium for 30 seconds
or until well whipped and smooth. Add the vanilla or peppermint extract and beat
again for at least 30 seconds or until smooth and whipped.

Add a drop of the pink gel coloring to the buttercream: dip a toothpick into the gel
and swirl the toothpick into the buttercream. Mix well on medium speed to evenly
distribute the color. If you want a deeper color, add more gel with a clean toothpick.
The amount of color you need will vary depending on the brand of color you use and
the depth of color saturation you prefer. Set aside at room temperature, or transfer to
an airtight container and refrigerate up to 5 days.

continued >>

To assemble the cake, gather together the cakes and buttercream. If you made the buttercream ahead and stored it in the refrigerator, be sure to bring it to room temperature and beat in the bowl of a stand mixer before proceeding. Split each cake in half horizontally (see page 173 for guidance). Spread $\frac{1}{2}$ cup buttercream between each cake layer, but do not frost the top or sides of the cake. Using an offset spatula or butter knife, wipe away any buttercream that extends beyond the edges of the layers, and refrigerate the cake until firm, about 1 hour. Cover the remaining buttercream with plastic wrap and set aside at room temperature.

While the cake chills, color and shape the white chocolate decor. Lightly grease your countertop with nonstick cooking spray. To avoid staining your hands with the food coloring, wear latex gloves. Transfer about three quarters of the white modeling chocolate from the plastic bag to the counter and knead the paste until pliable, about 1 minute. Using a toothpick, transfer a drop of pink gel coloring to the paste, and then knead to incorporate. Return one-half of this piece of modeling paste to the plastic bag. Roll the remaining pink paste to $\frac{1}{4}$-inch thickness. Using a crown-shaped cookie cutter (any size you have is fine; mine is 4 inches wide), cut out a single crown and transfer it to a parchment-lined baking sheet. If you want your crown to stand up (as shown in photo on page 135), prop it up and curve it around a glass or jar of appropriate size until it sets. Gather the pink scraps, knead them together, and add to the bag.

Using the reserved uncolored paste, roll about 50 small pearls and set aside with the crown on the baking sheet. Gather the scraps, knead them together, and set aside. You can always roll more beads if you'd like to add more to your cake. If preparing the decor more than 6 hours in advance of assembly, cover with plastic wrap and store at cool room temperature. The decor may be prepared up to 4 days ahead, but should not be refrigerated as it may suffer from condensation and bleed or turn soft.

The day you plan to serve it, decorate the cake: Frost the top and sides of the cake with the remaining buttercream, referring to page 173 for guidance, if necessary. Return the cake to the refrigerator to firm up for about 1 hour. The buttercream must be quite firm before you wrap the cake with the pink sheet and place the decor.

Roll out the remaining modeling paste to $\frac{1}{8}$-inch thickness and immediately use it to cover the cake, referring to the instructions on page 184. Next, lift your crown from the tray, using the tip of a knife to help release it, and cradle the crown in one palm to prevent stretching. Secure a pearl on each tip of the crown using pink buttercream. Center the crown on top of the cake and lightly press down with your palm. Using pink buttercream, affix additional pearls around the base and up the sides of the cake in a random pattern.

Store the cake at cool room temperature (tented with plastic wrap, if you like) until ready to serve. The cake will taste best served at room temperature.

Chocolate Cake batter (page 63)

**CHOCOLATE (BROWN)
BUTTERCREAM**

¾ cup (1½ sticks) unsalted butter
or nonhydrogenated vegetable
shortening, at room temperature

2 cups confectioners' sugar (to
make your own, see page 192)

¾ cup natural (nonalkalized)
cocoa powder

1 to 2 teaspoons milk or
unsweetened coconut milk
(from a carton)

**LIGHT CHOCOLATE (TAN)
BUTTERCREAM**

¾ cup (1½ sticks) unsalted butter
or nonhydrogenated vegetable
shortening, at room temperature

2½ cups confectioners' sugar

¼ cup natural (nonalkalized)
cocoa powder

1 to 2 teaspoons milk or
unsweetened coconut milk
(from a carton)

**VANILLA (GREEN)
BUTTERCREAM**

¾ cup (1½ sticks) unsalted butter
or nonhydrogenated vegetable
shortening, at room temperature

2¾ cups confectioners' sugar

2 teaspoons pure vanilla extract

Natural green gel food coloring

I first made a version of this chocolaty camo cake to celebrate the eighth birthday of my friend's son Will. Like so many kids, he was obsessed with those little plastic army men—and all things army—at the time. The cake was a huge hit, needless to say, with Will and all the kids at his party. The camo icing effect is achieved with three buttercream icings, two different tones of chocolate and one that's colored with natural green food coloring. I use PME Juniper Green 100 percent natural food coloring (see page 173). In place of the chocolate cake batter, you can use any type of cake batter from chapter 2—choose your little soldier's favorite.

Camo Cake

Preheat the oven to 350°F. To make the cake, lightly oil two 8-inch-diameter cake pans with nonstick cooking spray or coconut oil. Pour the batter into the prepared pans and bake as the recipe instructs, using a toothpick to test for doneness. Transfer the cakes to wire racks to cool for 10 minutes or until the pans are cool enough to handle safely, and then invert onto the racks to cool completely. You can make the cake layers ahead and freeze them, each tightly wrapped in a double layer of plastic wrap, for up to 1 month; thaw at room temperature before frosting the cake.

While the cakes bake and cool, make the buttercreams. You're going to use three buttercreams to create the camouflage effect: chocolate (dark brown), light chocolate (tan), and a green-tinted vanilla buttercream.

To make the chocolate (brown) buttercream: Beat the butter in the bowl of a stand mixer on high speed for 1 minute or until well whipped. Add the confectioners' sugar; cover most of your bowl with a kitchen towel to avoid a dust storm, and beat on low for 1 minute to combine. Add the cocoa powder and cover the bowl again; beat on low for 1 minute until combined, and then on medium for 1 minute or until well whipped. Add 1 teaspoon of the milk and beat on low to combine, and then whip on medium for 30 seconds or until smooth. Add the additional 1 teaspoon milk if necessary to achieve a spreadable consistency. Transfer the buttercream to a small bowl and cover with plastic wrap.

To make the light chocolate (tan) buttercream: Follow the same steps as above for the butter, confectioners' sugar, cocoa powder, and milk. Transfer the buttercream to a second small bowl and cover with plastic wrap.

To make the vanilla (green) buttercream: Beat the butter in the bowl of a stand mixer on high for 1 minute or until well whipped. Add the confectioners' sugar and vanilla extract and cover most of your bowl with a kitchen towel to avoid a dust storm; beat on low for 1 minute to combine, and then whip on medium for 30 seconds

continued on page 142 >>

Camo Cake (page 138)

Camo Cake,
continued >>

or until well whipped and smooth. Add the green food coloring, just a couple of drops at a time, until you achieve the desired color saturation. You want a light- to mid-tone green for the camouflage effect. Transfer the buttercream to a third small bowl and cover with plastic wrap.

To frost and assemble the cake, split each cake layer in half horizontally, following the procedure on page 173. Spread ¾ cup of the buttercream between each cake layer using a different color buttercream to fill each layer, but do not spread buttercream on the top or sides of the cake. Using an offset spatula or butter knife, wipe away any buttercream that extends beyond the edges of the layers, and chill the filled cake until firm, about 1 hour. Leave the remaining buttercream on the counter at room temperature, covered with plastic wrap.

Transfer the cake to the counter and gather the three buttercreams and a clean offset spatula or butter knife for each color of buttercream. Starting with the sides of the cake, create a small irregularly shaped patch with one color of buttercream, applying 2 to 3 tablespoons at a time and then smoothing out the frosting. Remember, you don't want to create a perfect geometric shape with sharp corners, you want to create more of an oddly shaped cloud. Apply the second and third colors in patches next to the first and repeat, working around the sides of the cake. Vary the size and shape of your patches. Frost the top of the cake in the same fashion.

Store the finished cake in an airtight container (or tented with plastic wrap) at cool room temperature up to 1 day, or in the refrigerator up to 2 days. The cake will taste best served at room temperature.

You can't get more whimsical than a polka-dotted party cake with a topper that bursts from the top of the cake like fireworks! It's a dessert that appeals to all ages, and depending on the color scheme you choose, it can appear youthful or elegant. If this is your first foray into a two-tiered cake, have no fear. If you follow my steps for stacking the tiers, you'll sail right through. You'll need two batches of cake and a biggie-size batch of buttercream, so consider baking the cake and preparing the buttercream a day or two ahead. Feel free to substitute another cake batter from chapter 2 and one of the big-batch buttercream flavor variations on page 156.

Two-Tiered Whimsy Cake

Make the white chocolate modeling paste through the kneading step according to the recipe instructions. Place the modeling paste in a resealable plastic bag and seal the bag. Let rest at cool room temperature at least 1 hour and up to 1 day. If the mixture is very sticky, place it on a piece of parchment paper and allow it to air-dry for 30 minutes before placing in the bag to rest.

Preheat the oven to 350°F. Lightly oil two 9-inch-diameter cake pans and two 6-inch-diameter cake pans with nonstick cooking spray or coconut oil. Pour the batter into the pans, filling them about half full. If you're making the coconut cake, bake the 9-inch cakes for 35 to 40 minutes and the 6-inch cakes for 20 to 25 minutes until the tops are light golden and a toothpick inserted into the center tests clean. (If you've selected another cake recipe, bake the 9-inch cakes about 5 minutes longer than indicated in the recipe and bake the 6-inch cakes 5 to 10 minutes less than indicated in the recipe.) Transfer the cakes to wire racks to cool for 10 minutes or until the cake pans are cool enough to handle, and then invert the cakes onto the racks to cool.

To fill and assemble the cake tiers, gather together the cake layers and buttercream. If you premade the buttercream and stored it in the refrigerator, bring it to room temperature and beat it in the bowl of a stand mixer before proceeding.

Split each cake layer in half horizontally to create four layers of each size, following the procedure on page 173. Place one 9-inch layer on a serving platter and top with about ½ cup buttercream. Spread out the buttercream to create a thin, even layer. Place the second layer on top, press down firmly, and repeat the buttercream filling application. Repeat the same steps for the remaining two layers, but do not spread buttercream on top of the final layer. Using an offset spatula or butter knife, wipe away any buttercream filling that extends beyond the edges of the layers, and place the large tier in the refrigerator to chill until the buttercream filling is firm, about 1 hour.

continued >>

MAKES ONE 6-INCH- AND ONE 9-INCH-DIAMETER CAKE TIER (22 TO 24 SERVINGS)

White Chocolate Modeling Paste (page 183)

Coconut Cake batter (page 51), recipe doubled

Big-Batch Coconut Buttercream (page 156)

Blue, pink, and yellow natural gel food coloring

SPECIAL TOOLS

Rolling pin

Small round cookie cutters

Plastic or latex gloves (optional)

One 6-inch-diameter corrugated cake cardboard

5 wooden dowels or heavy-duty straws

7 white floral wires

Repeat the process for the 6-inch layers, filling and assembling them separately from the 9-inch layers. Place about 1 tablespoon buttercream on top of the 6-inch tier, and then place the 6-inch corrugated cardboard on top of the cake. Press down so the buttercream "glue" adheres to the board. Turn the cake over so the board is now on the bottom of the tier. Place the small tier in the refrigerator to chill with the large tier until the buttercream filling is firm, about 1 hour. Cover the remaining buttercream with plastic wrap and let sit at cool room temperature.

While the cakes chill, color and shape the modeling paste decor. Lightly oil your countertop with nonstick cooking spray. Knead the white chocolate modeling paste on the counter until pliable, about 1 minute.

Divide the modeling chocolate into 3 pieces. Color each piece a different color: blue, pink, and yellow. It's a good idea to wear plastic or latex gloves. Use a toothpick to transfer a drop or two of the gel color to one piece of the modeling chocolate, and then knead to incorporate. It only takes a tiny bit of gel to achieve brilliant color. Repeat the process with the remaining 2 pieces of modeling paste and additional colors. The colored modeling chocolate will be used to make polka dots for the side of the cake and balls for the topper. Wrap tightly in plastic wrap and store in a reseable plastic bag.

To make the whimsy topper, cut 7 floral wires into roughly 4-inch lengths. Pinch off 7 tiny pieces of the modeling paste (use one color or a mix of colors) and roll the pieces between your palms to create balls approximately the diameter of a pearl earring. Insert a floral wire into each of the 7 balls, pressing the wire only about halfway into the ball. Briefly set the wired balls aside on a parchment-lined baking sheet.

To make the base for the topper, pinch off another piece of paste, about three times the size of the other balls, and roll a ball. Flatten this larger ball slightly on the bottom so that it will not roll around, and place it on the sheet. Insert the whimsy wires into the base, placing one wire straight up in the center and the others at jaunty angles around the center wire. Your topper is now complete.

To make the polka dots, you can use any small, round cookie cutters. I used a 1-inch cutter and the back end of a small metal piping tip, which measured about $\frac{1}{2}$ inch. Make just one size polka dot or two or three sizes for a more whimsical effect. Using a rolling pin, roll out each color of the remaining modeling paste to $\frac{1}{8}$-inch thickness. Using your small, round cookie cutters, cut between 15 and 35 dots, depending on the size of your cutters and how many dots you want to have on your cake. Place the dots on a parchment-lined baking sheet, cover them with plastic wrap so they remain flexible, and set the tray aside at cool room temperature until you're ready to decorate your cake. All the decor may be prepared up to 4 days before assembly.

To frost the cake tiers, reserve 2 tablespoons of the buttercream for stacking the cake tiers. Frost the tops and sides of both tiers with the remaining buttercream (see page 173). Return the frosted cakes to the refrigerator to firm up, at least 1 hour. You'll want the buttercream quite firm before you stack the tiers.

To assemble and decorate the cake, after the frosted cakes have chilled, bring the 9-inch cake tier to the counter, leaving the 6-inch tier in the refrigerator. Gather together the dowels or straws and something to cut them with (scissors for the straws and wire snips or garden pruners for the dowels), along with a clean, dry 6-inch-diameter cake pan, a paring knife, and the reserved 2 tablespoons of buttercream.

Gently place the cake pan so it's centered on top of the 9-inch cake tier. Lightly run the tip of the paring knife around the base of the pan, exactly where you want the 6-inch cake tier to sit. Insert one dowel or straw into the center of the cake in the middle of the tracing, pushing the dowel to the cake plate. Grasp the dowel with two fingers and use your thumb to mark the point where the icing meets the dowel; remove the dowel and cut with the wire snips or garden pruners. Lay the cut dowel on the counter and place an uncut dowel next to it. Cut the second dowel to match the length of the cut dowel. Repeat with the remaining dowels until all five are the same length.

Insert one dowel into the center of the cake. Place the four remaining dowels around the central dowel to form a square; the four corners should be $\frac{1}{2}$ inch inside of the tracing of the pan you made with the paring knife. Using the reserved 2 tablespoons of buttercream, spread a very thin layer of icing "glue" over the tops of the dowels to cover the tracing area. Do not extend the icing beyond the tracing area.

Remove the 6-inch cake tier from the refrigerator. Using a spatula and your fingertips, take the smaller cake tier off the cardboard and place it atop the larger one, lining up the top tier with the tracing. (You can cover any fingerprints or indentations with your dots.)

Place the dots on the sides of the cake in a random fashion. If the buttercream has formed a firm crust and the dots won't adhere, use the tiniest bit of water to make the back of each dot tacky. Center the whimsy topper on the top of the cake.

Keep the cake at cool room temperature (tented in plastic wrap, if you like) until ready to serve, up to 1 day. The cake will taste best served at room temperature. You can make the frosted cakes up to 2 days in advance, but don't apply modeling chocolate decor until the day you plan to serve the cake. The decor should not be refrigerated, as it may suffer from condensation and bleed or turn soft.

White Chocolate Modeling
Paste (page 183), recipe doubled

Chocolate Cake batter (page 63)

ORANGE BUTTERCREAM

1 cup (2 sticks) unsalted butter
or nonhydrogenated vegetable
shortening, at room temperature

3½ cups confectioners' sugar
(to make your own, see page 192)

2 teaspoons freshly squeezed
orange juice

Orange natural gel food coloring

Natural gel food coloring, your
choice of color, for the eyes

SPECIAL TOOLS

Rolling pin

Plastic or latex gloves (optional)

Halloween is chock-full of treats, but almost all are loaded with gluten. I created this cake so everyone can share in the creepy fun—and what could be more creepy (and fun) than a mummy? The technique of layering the modeling chocolate "mummy bandages" is surprisingly simple and very effective. Encourage your children to help you decorate, and don't worry about making it look perfect. A few strips of modeling chocolate hanging loose is exactly what you want: it should look as if the mummy is about to burst out of his wraps and join the party!

Fright Night Mummy Cake

Make the white chocolate modeling paste through the kneading step according to the instructions. Transfer to a resealable plastic bag and seal the bag. Let rest at cool room temperature at least 1 hour and up to 1 day. If the mixture is very sticky, place it on a piece of parchment paper and allow it to air-dry for 30 minutes before placing it in the bag to rest.

Preheat the oven to 350°F. Lightly oil two 8-inch-diameter cake pans with nonstick cooking spray or coconut oil. Pour the batter into the prepared pans and bake as the recipe instructs, using a toothpick to test for doneness. Transfer the cakes to wire racks to cool for 10 minutes or until the pans are cool enough to handle safely, and then invert onto the racks to cool completely. You can freeze the cake layers, each tightly wrapped in plastic wrap, up to 1 month; thaw at room temperature before frosting and decorating the cake.

While the cakes bake and cool, make the buttercream: In the bowl of a stand mixer with the paddle attachment, beat the butter on high speed for 1 minute until well whipped. Add the confectioners' sugar and cover most of your bowl with a kitchen towel to avoid a dust storm; beat on low for 1 minute to combine, and then whip on medium for 30 seconds or until well whipped and smooth. Add the orange juice and beat again for at least 30 seconds or until smooth and whipped.

Dip a toothpick into the orange gel coloring, and swirl the toothpick into the buttercream. Mix well on medium speed to evenly distribute the color. If you want a deeper color, add more gel using a clean toothpick. The amount of color you need will vary depending on the brand of color you use and the depth of color saturation you prefer. Set aside at cool room temperature while you assemble and decorate the cake, or transfer the buttercream to an airtight container and refrigerate up to 5 days. Bring the buttercream to room temperature and beat it in the bowl of a stand mixer to restore its texture before continuing.

To frost and assemble the cake, split each cake layer in half horizontally, following the procedure on page 173. Spread ½ cup buttercream between each cake layer, but do not frost the top or sides of the cake. Using an offset spatula or butter knife, wipe away any buttercream that extends beyond the edges of the layers, and then refrigerate the cake to chill until firm, about 1 hour. Leave the remaining buttercream on the counter at cool room temperature, covered with plastic wrap. At this stage, you can keep the cake in the refrigerator up to 2 days. Refrigerate the remaining buttercream and restore its texture as described above before using.

While the cake chills, make the modeling chocolate eyeballs. Remove a small amount of the white chocolate modeling paste from the plastic bag, enough to make 2 eyeballs, each just a bit smaller than a golf ball. Leave the remaining paste in the bag.

Lightly grease your countertop with nonstick cooking spray and knead the piece of paste until pliable, about 1 minute. Pinch off enough for two pea-size pieces of modeling chocolate and set aside; this will be used to make the pupils of the eyes. Divide the remaining paste in half and roll into 2 balls for the eyeballs. Set aside while you color the paste for the pupils.

Using a gel color of your choice, color the piece reserved for the pupils. Green or blue works well. Dip a toothpick into the gel, transfer a drop or two of the gel onto the paste, and knead to evenly distribute the color. Your hands may become stained, so it's a good idea to wear plastic or latex gloves. Divide the colored paste in half and roll 2 small beads. Flatten each bead into a disk and gently press one disk onto each eyeball to create the eyes. Set the eyes aside until ready to decorate the cake. If preparing the eyeballs more than 6 hours in advance, wrap loosely in plastic wrap and store at cool room temperature. The eyeballs may be prepared up to 4 days before assembly.

Remove the chilled cake from the refrigerator and, using a spatula and your hand, transfer it to a large piece of parchment paper on the counter. Using a serrated bread knife, cut off the top edge of the cake at a 45-degree angle to create a gentle slope around the top of the cake. The angle does not need to be perfectly consistent, just be sure you remove the sharp top edges of the cake. Frost the top and sides of cake with the remaining buttercream, referring to page 173 for guidance. Return the cake to the refrigerator to firm up for about 30 minutes.

When ready to decorate, gather together the cake, modeling paste eyeballs, and remaining modeling paste. Remove the modeling paste from the plastic bag and knead until pliable, about 1 minute. Roll out the paste to $\frac{1}{8}$-inch thickness and cut strips of "mummy wrap," in any length and width that you're comfortable handling. (I use $\frac{3}{4}$-inch-wide strips that measure 6 to 10 inches in length.)

Pressing gently to make them stick, place the eyeballs on the top of the cake, just slightly above the centerline, where eyeballs would be on a face. Then lay the strips of modeling paste over the cake to create the mummy wrapping, leaving the eyeballs exposed. Overlap the strips and leave some of them askew so the mummy looks disheveled.

Store the finished cake in an airtight container (or tented with plastic wrap) at cool room temperature until ready to serve, up to 1 day. The cake will taste best served at room temperature. The decor should not be refrigerated as it may suffer from condensation and bleed or turn soft.

White Chocolate Modeling
Paste (page 183), recipe halved

PUMPKIN ROULADE CAKE

¾ cup Gluten-Free All-Purpose
Flour Blend (page 191), plus
additional for sprinkling

1 cup organic cane sugar

1 tablespoon plus 1 teaspoon
pumpkin pie spice

½ teaspoon xanthan gum

½ teaspoon baking powder

½ teaspoon baking soda

¼ teaspoon fine sea salt

3 eggs, lightly beaten, at room
temperature

⅔ cup canned pumpkin puree
(not pumpkin pie filling)

¼ cup confectioners' sugar, for
sprinkling (to make your own,
see page 192)

Almond Buttercream (page 156)

Edible glitter flakes (optional)

Beaten egg white, for adhering
the glitter (optional)

SPECIAL TOOLS

Rolling pin

Lint-free tea towel for rolling
the roulade

Small snowflake-shaped
cookie cutter

Typically, this beloved French holiday dessert is iced in chocolate and covered in meringue "mushrooms" to resemble the historical Yule log that was used in northern European fireplaces to cook the Christmas Eve dinner. My version pays tribute to my childhood white Christmases in Connecticut, and takes full advantage of my favorite holiday flavors—pumpkin and almond. The almond buttercream provides the perfect backdrop for the shimmering white chocolate snowflakes, which appear to have just fallen from the sky for a white (and gluten-free) Christmas. The cake roll is easier to prepare than you might think. Simply follow my step-by-step instructions and don't worry if you get a few cracks; they'll be covered up by the icing.

White Christmas Bûche de Noël

Make the white chocolate modeling paste through the kneading step according to the instructions on page 183. Place the modeling paste in a resealable plastic bag and seal the bag. Let rest at cool room temperature at least 1 hour and up to 1 day. If the mixture is very sticky, place it on a piece of parchment paper and allow it to air-dry for 30 minutes before placing in the bag to rest.

To make the cake: Preheat the oven to 375°F. Lightly oil a 13 by 18-inch jelly-roll pan with nonstick cooking spray and line it with parchment paper. Lightly oil the paper, sprinkle with some flour, and tap the pan to evenly distribute the flour. Set aside.

In the bowl of a stand mixer with the paddle attachment, combine the sugar, flour blend, pumpkin pie spice, xanthan gum, baking powder, baking soda, and salt. Mix on low speed for 30 seconds, just to combine. Add the eggs and pumpkin puree and beat on medium for 1 minute until well blended (the batter will be thin).

Pour the batter into the prepared pan and spread it evenly using an offset spatula or the back of a large spoon. Bang the pan on the counter to release any air bubbles. (Bang it hard, it's fun!) Bake in the center of the oven for about 15 minutes, until the top springs back when touched. You don't want to underbake this cake or it will be a sticky mess to work with.

While the cake is baking, spread out a tea towel on your counter and sprinkle it with the confectioners' sugar. When the cake has finished baking, immediately turn it out onto the prepared towel. Peel the parchment from the bottom of the cake and position the cake so the short edge faces you. Using the short edge of the tea towel, roll up the cake completely using the towel to guide you, rolling the towel inside the cake (don't worry, we'll take it out later!). Set aside on a wire rack to cool completely.

continued >>

White Christmas Bûche de Nöel,
continued >>

To fill and roll the cake, when the cake is completely cool to the touch, carefully unroll it. Spread about two-thirds of the buttercream evenly over the cake, leaving a 1-inch gap around the edge. Reroll the cake, this time without the tea towel; wrap tightly in plastic wrap and refrigerate at least 2 hours and up to 2 days. Or you can freeze the cake in a double layer of plastic wrap up to 1 month; thaw overnight in the refrigerator, until the cake is no longer frozen but still chilled, before continuing.

While the cake chills, make the white chocolate modeling paste decor. Lightly grease your countertop with nonstick cooking spray, transfer the modeling chocolate from the plastic bag to the counter, and knead until pliable, about 1 minute. Roll the modeling paste to $\frac{1}{4}$-inch thickness.

Using your small snowflake cookie cutter, cut 8 to 10 snowflakes out of the modeling chocolate. If using the optional glitter flakes, dredge the snowflakes in the glitter while they are still tacky, and then set them aside on a parchment-lined baking sheet. If the glitter does not want to stick to your snowflakes, use a very small amount of egg white to dampen the snowflakes with your finger before dredging.

To decorate the cake, transfer the roll from the fridge to your countertop and remove the plastic wrap. Using a sharp knife, cut off the ragged edges of the roll and place the roll on a serving platter. Frost the cake with the remaining buttercream, completely covering the roll. Use the tip of a spoon or a butter knife to drag barklike channels through the buttercream down the length of the "log." Place the snowflakes on the top and sides of the cake in a random fashion, gently pressing to help them adhere. Any extra flakes can be scattered on the serving platter.

Keep the cake at cool room temperature (tented in plastic wrap, if you like) until ready to serve, up to 1 day. The cake will taste best served at room temperature. The decor should not be refrigerated or frozen as it may suffer from condensation and bleed or turn soft.

TIP

As you're sure to be busy come holiday time, you can prepare the filled and rolled-up cake up to 1 month ahead and keep it in the freezer until the day before your party. Just transfer the cake to the countertop to thaw, and then ice and decorate with your snowflakes.

ESSENTIAL FROSTINGS, FILLINGS
& glazes

From a Chocolate Hazelnut Buttercream (page 158) and Caramel Filling (page 164) to an Ancho Cinnamon Ganache (page 162), here are irresistible recipes for the frostings, fillings, and glazes essential to many of the cake recipes in this book. They are luscious slathered or piped on the cakes that I suggest, but also offer you a chance to play pastry chef. Feel free to mix and match the cakes, fillings, and glazes to invent your own cake and cupcake masterpieces. The cake recipes can become entirely new creations simply by switching one flavor of buttercream for another—or by using a smooth ganache instead of a thick and fudgy frosting.

Buttercreams should be covered with plastic wrap and kept at cool room temperature until you're ready to use them. You can refrigerate the buttercreams and icings in an airtight container for up to five days or freeze for a month. Bring to room temperature and beat in the bowl of a stand mixer to restore the proper texture before using.

Ganaches (and caramel filling) must be cooled to room temperature before using, unless otherwise noted. You can refrigerate the ganaches in an airtight container up to one week. Bring to room temperature before using unless otherwise instructed. For the glazes, follow the instructions in each cake recipe concerning appropriate temperature.

Almond Buttercream

MAKES 3½ CUPS

1 cup (2 sticks) unsalted butter or nonhydrogenated vegetable shortening, at room temperature

3 cups confectioners' sugar

1 to 2 teaspoons pure almond extract

In the bowl of a stand mixer with the paddle attachment, beat the butter on high for 1 minute or until lightened and whipped. Add the confectioners' sugar, cover most of your bowl with a kitchen towel to avoid a dust storm, and beat on low for 1 minute to combine. Add 1 teaspoon almond extract and combine on low. Taste and add up to 1 teaspoon additional almond extract if desired (some brands have stronger flavors than others). Combine on low and then beat on medium for 30 seconds more or until well whipped and smooth.

Big-Batch Coconut Buttercream

MAKES 7 CUPS

2 cups (4 sticks) unsalted butter or nonhydrogenated vegetable shortening, at room temperature

7 cups confectioners' sugar

1 to 2 teaspoons pure coconut extract

Make the buttercream in two batches (a home mixer won't accommodate the full yield). In the bowl of a stand mixer with the paddle attachment, beat 1 cup (2 sticks) of the butter on high speed for 1 minute until lightened and whipped. Add 3½ cups of the confectioners' sugar, and cover most of your bowl with a kitchen towel to avoid a dust storm; beat on low for 1 minute to combine, and then beat on medium for 30 seconds or until well whipped and smooth. Add 1 teaspoon of the coconut extract (or optional flavoring of choice; see below) and beat again for 30 seconds or until smooth and whipped. Transfer the buttercream to a large bowl and make the second batch. Add the second batch to the buttercream in the bowl; taste and mix in a little more coconut extract if desired.

VARIATIONS

To switch up the flavor of the big-batch buttercream recipe above, swap the 1 to 2 teaspoons of pure coconut extract in the recipe above for the following:

Very Vanilla: 2 teaspoons pure vanilla extract

Lemon: 2 teaspoons freshly squeezed lemon juice

Orange: 2 teaspoons freshly squeezed orange juice

Almond: 1 to 2 teaspoons pure almond extract

Caramel: 2 tablespoons cooled caramel (store-bought or homemade, page 164) plus 1 teaspoon pure vanilla extract

Peppermint: 1 teaspoon pure peppermint extract

Caramel Buttercream

MAKES 3½ CUPS

1 cup (2 sticks) unsalted butter or nonhydrogenated vegetable shortening, at room temperature

3 cups confectioners' sugar

⅓ cup lightly packed light brown sugar

2 tablespoons cooled Caramel Filling (page 164) or store-bought caramel sauce

1 teaspoon pure vanilla extract

In the bowl of a stand mixer with the paddle attachment, beat the butter on high for 1 minute until well whipped. Add the confectioners' sugar and brown sugar, cover most of the bowl with a kitchen towel to avoid a dust storm, and beat on low for 1 minute to combine. Add the caramel and vanilla; combine on low speed, and then beat on medium for 30 seconds more or until well whipped and smooth.

Chocolate Buttercream

MAKES 3½ TO 4 CUPS

1 cup (2 sticks) unsalted butter or nonhydrogenated vegetable shortening, at room temperature

3 cups confectioners' sugar

⅔ cup natural (nonalkalized) cocoa powder

1 tablespoon milk or unsweetened coconut milk (from a carton)

In the bowl of a stand mixer, beat the butter on high for 1 minute until well whipped. Add the confectioners' sugar, cover most of your bowl with a kitchen towel to avoid a dust storm, and beat on low for 1 minute to combine. Add the cocoa powder, cover your bowl again, and beat on low for 1 minute to combine, and then on medium for 1 minute or until well whipped. Add the milk; beat on low to combine, and then beat on medium for 30 seconds more or until well whipped and smooth.

Chocolate Ganache Buttercream

MAKES 3¾ TO 4 CUPS

1 cup (2 sticks) unsalted butter or nonhydrogenated vegetable shortening, at room temperature

3 cups confectioners' sugar

⅔ cup natural (nonalkalized) cocoa powder

1 tablespoon milk or unsweetened coconut milk (from a carton)

¼ cup cooled Chocolate Ganache (page 162)

In the bowl of a stand mixer, beat the butter on high for 1 minute until well whipped. Add the confectioners' sugar, cover most of your bowl with a kitchen towel to avoid a dust storm, and beat on low for 1 minute to combine. Add the cocoa powder, cover your bowl again, and beat on low for 1 minute to combine, and then on medium for 1 minute or until well whipped. Add the milk and ganache and beat on low to combine, and then on medium for 30 seconds more or until well whipped and smooth.

Chocolate Hazelnut Buttercream

MAKES 3½ CUPS

1 cup (2 sticks) unsalted butter or nonhydrogenated vegetable shortening, at room temperature

3 cups confectioners' sugar

⅔ cup natural (nonalkalized) cocoa powder, or more to taste

1 tablespoon milk or canned unsweetened coconut milk

2 teaspoons pure vanilla extract

2 tablespoons Nutella or dairy-free chocolate hazelnut spread

In the bowl of a stand mixer with the paddle attachment, beat the butter on high for 1 minute or until lightened and whipped. Add the confectioners' sugar, cover most of your bowl with a kitchen towel, and beat on low for 1 minute to combine. Add the cocoa powder, cover the bowl again, and beat on low for 1 minute to combine, and then on medium for 1 minute. Taste and if you want more chocolate flavor, add up to 2 tablespoons additional cocoa. Beat to combine. Add the milk and combine on low, and then beat on medium for 30 seconds until well whipped. Add the vanilla and Nutella and beat again for 1 minute until smooth and fluffy.

Cinnamon Maple Buttercream

MAKES 3½ CUPS

1 cup (2 sticks) unsalted butter or nonhydrogenated vegetable shortening, at room temperature

3½ cups confectioners' sugar

2 teaspoons pure vanilla extract

2 teaspoons maple syrup

2 teaspoons ground cinnamon

In the bowl of a stand mixer with the paddle attachment, beat the butter on high for 1 minute until well whipped. Add the confectioners' sugar, vanilla, maple syrup, and cinnamon. Cover most of your bowl with a kitchen towel to avoid a dust storm; beat on low for 1 minute to combine, and then beat on medium for 30 seconds more or until well whipped and smooth.

Coconut Buttercream

MAKES 3½ CUPS

1 cup (2 sticks) unsalted butter or nonhydrogenated vegetable shortening, at room temperature

3½ cups confectioners' sugar

1 to 2 teaspoons pure coconut extract

In the bowl of a stand mixer with the paddle attachment, beat the butter on high for 1 minute until lightened and whipped. Add the confectioners' sugar and 1 teaspoon of the coconut extract, cover most of your bowl with a kitchen towel to avoid a dust storm, and beat on low for 1 minute to combine. Beat on medium for 30 seconds more or until well whipped and smooth. Taste and add up to 1 teaspoon additional coconut extract, if desired. Whip to combine.

Espresso Buttercream

MAKES 3½ CUPS

1 cup (2 sticks) unsalted butter or nonhydrogenated vegetable shortening, at room temperature

4 cups confectioners' sugar

1 teaspoon pure vanilla extract

4 teaspoons instant espresso powder

2 teaspoons milk or unsweetened coconut milk (from a carton)

In the bowl of a stand mixer with the paddle attachment, beat the butter on high speed for 1 minute or until well whipped. Add the confectioners' sugar, cover most of your bowl with a kitchen towel to avoid a dust storm, and beat on low for 1 minute to combine. Add the vanilla and mix on low for 30 seconds. Combine the espresso powder and milk in a small bowl or cup and stir together to form a smooth paste. Add the espresso paste to the buttercream and beat on medium for 30 seconds or until well whipped and smooth.

Lemon Buttercream

MAKES 3½ CUPS

1 cup (2 sticks) unsalted butter or nonhydrogenated vegetable shortening, at room temperature

3 cups confectioners' sugar

1 tablespoon freshly squeezed lemon juice

2 teaspoons organic lemon zest (optional)

In the bowl of a stand mixer with the paddle attachment, beat the butter on high for 1 minute or until well whipped. Add the confectioners' sugar, cover most of your bowl with a kitchen towel to avoid a dust storm, and beat on low for 1 minute to combine. Add the lemon juice and zest; combine on low, and then beat on medium for 30 seconds more or until well whipped and smooth.

Peppermint Buttercream

MAKES 3½ CUPS

1 cup (2 sticks) unsalted butter or nonhydrogenated vegetable shortening, at room temperature

3½ cups confectioners' sugar

1 teaspoon pure peppermint extract

In the bowl of a stand mixer with the paddle attachment, beat the butter on high speed for 1 minute until well whipped. Add the confectioners' sugar and peppermint extract, cover most of your bowl with a kitchen towel to avoid a dust storm, and beat on low for 1 minute to combine. Scrape down the bowl using a rubber spatula. Beat on medium for 1 minute more or until light and fluffy.

Strawberry Buttercream

MAKES 3½ CUPS

1 cup (2 sticks) unsalted butter or nonhydrogenated vegetable shortening, at room temperature

3½ cups confectioners' sugar

¼ to ½ cup cooled Strawberry Puree (page 52)

In the bowl of a stand mixer with the paddle attachment, beat the butter on high for 1 minute until lightened and whipped. Add the confectioners' sugar, cover most of your bowl with a kitchen towel to avoid a dust storm, and beat on low for 1 minute to combine. Beat on medium for 1 minute medium more, and then scrape down the bowl. Add ¼ cup of the cooled strawberry puree and beat until well combined. Taste the buttercream and, if a deeper flavor and color are desired, add up to ¼ cup additional puree. Whip to combine.

Peanut Butter Buttercream

MAKES 3½ CUPS

1 cup (2 sticks) unsalted butter or nonhydrogenated vegetable shortening, at room temperature

3½ cups confectioners' sugar

½ cup creamy natural peanut butter

1 teaspoon pure vanilla extract

2 teaspoons fine sea salt

In the bowl of a stand mixer with the paddle attachment, beat the butter on high speed for 1 minute until well whipped. Add the confectioners' sugar, cover most of your bowl with a kitchen towel to avoid a dust storm, and beat on low for 1 minute until combined. Add the peanut butter, vanilla, and salt and mix on low to combine, then beat on medium for 30 seconds more or until well whipped and smooth. Taste and add more salt, if necessary, to balance the sweetness and bring out the peanut butter flavor. Whip to combine.

Very Vanilla Buttercream

MAKES 3½ CUPS

1 cup (2 sticks) unsalted butter or nonhydrogenated vegetable shortening, at room temperature

3½ cups confectioners' sugar

2 teaspoons pure vanilla extract

2 teaspoons vanilla bean paste (optional but oh-so-good; see page 196)

In the bowl of a stand mixer with the paddle attachment, beat the butter on high for 1 minute or until lightened and whipped. Add the confectioners' sugar, vanilla extract, and vanilla bean paste and cover most of your bowl with a kitchen towel to avoid a dust storm. Beat on low for 1 minute to combine, and then beat on medium for 30 seconds more or until well whipped and smooth.

Salted Caramel Buttercream

MAKES 3½ CUPS

1 cup (2 sticks) unsalted butter or nonhydrogenated vegetable shortening, at room temperature

3 cups confectioners' sugar

⅓ cup lightly packed light brown sugar

2 tablespoons cooled Caramel Filling (page 164) or store-bought salted caramel sauce

1 teaspoon pure vanilla extract

1 teaspoon fine sea salt

In the bowl of a stand mixer with the paddle attachment, beat the butter on high for 1 minute or until well whipped. Add the confectioners' sugar and brown sugar; cover most of your bowl with a kitchen towel to avoid a dust storm, and beat on low for 1 minute to combine. Add the caramel, vanilla, and salt. Mix on low to combine, and then beat on medium for 30 seconds more or until well whipped and smooth. You can refrigerate the buttercream and filling in an airtight container for 5 days or freeze for 1 month. Bring to room temperature and beat in the bowl of a stand mixer to restore proper texture before using.

Ancho Cinnamon Ganache

MAKES 3 CUPS

2 cups dark chocolate chips

2 cups heavy cream or canned unsweetened coconut milk (shake cans before opening)

1 to 2 teaspoons ground cinnamon

1 to 2 teaspoons ancho chile powder

Place the chocolate in a shallow heatproof bowl. In a small saucepan, bring the cream to a simmer. Pour the cream over the chocolate chips and shake the bowl to submerge the chocolate. Allow the mixture to sit for 1 minute undisturbed, and then whisk until smooth. Add 1 teaspoon each of the cinnamon and chile powder, whisking until smooth. Taste and add up to 1 teaspoon more of each, if desired.

Chocolate Ganache

MAKES 3 CUPS

2 cups dark chocolate chips

2 cups heavy cream or canned unsweetened coconut milk (shake cans before opening)

Place the chocolate chips in a shallow, heatproof bowl. In a small saucepan, bring the cream to a simmer. Pour the simmering cream over the chocolate chips, shaking the bowl to submerge the chocolate. Allow the mixture to sit for 1 minute undisturbed, then whisk until smooth. Set aside to cool completely.

Chocolate Cherry Ganache

MAKES 3 CUPS

2 cups dark chocolate chips

2 cups heavy cream or canned unsweetened coconut milk (shake cans before opening)

1 to 2 teaspoons kirsch

Place the chocolate chips in a shallow, heatproof bowl. In a small saucepan, bring the cream to a simmer. Pour the simmering cream over the chocolate chips, shaking the bowl to submerge the chocolate. Allow the mixture to sit for 1 minute undisturbed, and then whisk until smooth. Add 1 teaspoon kirsch, and if a more intense flavor is desired, add up to 1 teaspoon more, whisking to combine. Set aside to cool completely.

Chocolate Hazelnut Ganache

MAKES 3 CUPS

2 cups dark chocolate chips

2 cups heavy cream or canned unsweetened coconut milk (shake cans before opening)

¼ cup Nutella or dairy-free chocolate hazelnut spread

Place the chocolate chips in a shallow heatproof bowl. In a small saucepan, bring the cream to a simmer. Pour the simmering cream over the chocolate chips, shaking the bowl to submerge the chocolate. Allow the mixture to sit for 1 minute undisturbed, and then whisk until smooth. Add the Nutella and whisk until smooth. Set aside to cool completely.

Chocolate Peppermint Ganache

MAKES 3 CUPS

2 cups dark chocolate chips

2 cups heavy cream or canned unsweetened coconut milk (shake cans before opening)

1 teaspoon pure peppermint extract

Place the chocolate chips in a shallow, heatproof bowl. In a small saucepan, bring the cream to a simmer. Pour the simmering cream over the chocolate chips, shaking the bowl to submerge the chocolate. Allow the mixture to sit for 1 minute undisturbed, and then whisk until smooth. Add the peppermint extract and whisk again until smooth. Cover and refrigerate until thick enough to spread, about 20 minutes.

Orange Chocolate Ganache

MAKES 3 CUPS

2 cups dark chocolate chips

2 cups heavy cream or canned unsweetened coconut milk (shake cans before opening)

2 tablespoons freshly squeezed orange juice

1 tablespoon organic orange zest

Place the chocolate chips in a shallow heatproof bowl. In a small saucepan, bring the cream and orange juice to a simmer. Pour the simmering cream mixture over the chocolate chips and shake the bowl to submerge the chocolate. Allow the mixture to sit for 1 minute undisturbed, and then whisk until smooth. Add the orange zest and whisk again. Cover and refrigerate until thick enough to spread, about 20 minutes.

White Chocolate Ganache

MAKES 2 CUPS

2 cups white chocolate chips

1¼ cups heavy cream

Place the chocolate chips in a shallow, heatproof bowl. In a small saucepan, bring the cream to a simmer. Pour the simmering cream over the chocolate chips, shaking the bowl to submerge the chocolate. Allow the mixture to sit for 1 minute, undisturbed, then whisk until smooth. Set aside to cool completely.

Glossy Chocolate Glaze

MAKES 3 CUPS

½ cup dark chocolate chips

½ cup heavy cream or canned unsweetened coconut milk (shake the can before opening)

2 tablespoons raw honey or light agave nectar

Place the chocolate chips in a small heatproof bowl. In a small saucepan, bring the cream to a simmer. Pour the hot cream over the chocolate, shaking the bowl to submerge the chocolate. Allow the mixture to sit for 1 minute undisturbed, and then add the honey and whisk to create a smooth, pourable glaze.

Espresso Cinnamon Glaze

MAKES ½ CUP

½ cup canned unsweetened coconut milk (shake can before opening)

2 tablespoons confectioners' sugar

½ teaspoon ground cinnamon

½ teaspoon pure vanilla extract

1 to 2 teaspoons instant espresso powder (see page 196)

In a small bowl, whisk together the coconut milk, confectioners' sugar, cinnamon, vanilla, and espresso powder, to taste, until it is a smooth, pourable glaze.

Caramel Filling

MAKES 1 CUP

1½ cups heavy cream or canned unsweetened coconut milk

¾ cup organic cane sugar

½ teaspoon fine sea salt

Combine the cream, sugar, and salt in a heavy-bottomed medium saucepan. Use a pan that's larger than you think you'll need, as the caramel may bubble up vigorously. Bring the cream and sugar mixture to a boil over medium-high heat, stirring occasionally with a long-handled whisk or wooden spoon. Continue boiling and stirring carefully until the caramel darkens in color and thickens, about 15 minutes. Remove the caramel from the heat and let cool for about 10 minutes. Pour it into a clean bowl and cool completely.

Chocolate Icing

MAKES 3 CUPS

1 cup (2 sticks) unsalted butter or Earth Balance Vegan Buttery Sticks

½ cup natural (nonalkalized) cocoa powder

½ cup milk or unsweetened coconut milk (from a carton)

2 teaspoons pure vanilla extract

4¼ cups confectioners' sugar

Melt the butter in a large saucepan over medium heat. Add the cocoa powder and whisk to combine. Reduce the heat to low. Add the milk, vanilla, and confectioners' sugar in two batches, whisking to create a smooth, pourable icing.

Swiss Meringue Icing

MAKES 7 CUPS

1 cup egg whites (about 8 large whites), at room temperature

1¾ cups organic cane sugar

⅛ teaspoon fine sea salt

Place a clean, shallow stainless steel bowl on top of a saucepan filled with 2 inches of water and bring to a boil. Whisk together the egg whites, sugar, and salt in the bowl. Continue whisking until the whites are very hot to the touch, 5 to 7 minutes. Immediately transfer the mixture to the bowl of a stand mixer fitted with a whisk attachment and beat on high until glossy. The meringue should hold stiff peaks when the whisk is lifted.

Brown Sugar and Cinnamon Cream Cheese Icing

MAKES 3 CUPS

8 ounces cream cheese or dairy-free cream cheese, at room temperature

4 tablespoons unsalted butter or nonhydrogenated vegetable shortening, at room temperature

2 cups confectioners' sugar

⅓ cup lightly packed light brown sugar

1 teaspoon pure vanilla extract

1 teaspoon ground cinnamon

In the bowl of a stand mixer with the paddle attachment, beat the cream cheese and butter on high until light and fluffy. Add the confectioners' sugar, brown sugar, vanilla, and cinnamon. Cover most of your bowl with a kitchen towel to avoid a sugar dust storm; beat on low to combine, and then on medium-high for 2 minutes more or until light and fluffy.

White Chocolate Cream Cheese Icing

MAKES 3 CUPS

8 ounces cream cheese or dairy-free cream cheese, at room temperature

4 tablespoons unsalted butter or nonhydrogenated vegetable shortening, at room temperature

2½ cups confectioners' sugar

⅓ cup white chocolate chips, melted and cooled to lukewarm (see Tip)

1 teaspoon pure vanilla extract

In the bowl of a stand mixer with the paddle attachment, beat the cream cheese and butter on high for 1 minute until well whipped. Add the confectioners' sugar, cooled white chocolate, and vanilla and cover most of your bowl with a kitchen towel to avoid a dust storm. Beat on low for 1 minute to combine, and then beat on medium for 30 seconds. Scrape down the bowl and beat on medium for 1 minute more or until light and fluffy.

TIPS

White chocolate is more heat sensitive than dark or milk chocolate. Melt it in a stainless steel bowl placed over a saucepan containing 1 inch of simmering water. Once the water simmers, remove the pan from the heat, leaving the bowl atop the pan, and allow the white chocolate to sit for 1 minute to melt. Gently stir until completely melted and smooth.

If you use vegan cream cheese for either cream cheese icing, you'll want to chill the icing before using it to help it set up.

Fudgy Frosting

MAKES 4 CUPS

¾ cup (1½ sticks) unsalted butter or
Earth Balance Vegan Buttery Sticks

½ cup organic cane sugar

¾ cup canned unsweetened coconut
milk (shake can before opening)

3 teaspoons instant espresso powder
(optional; see page 196)

6 ounces unsweetened
baking chocolate

⅔ cup dark or semisweet chocolate chips

1 teaspoon pure vanilla extract

2¼ cups confectioners' sugar

In a medium saucepan over medium heat, combine the butter,
sugar, coconut milk, and espresso powder, stirring until the
butter melts and the sugar and espresso have dissolved. Bring
to a simmer, and then remove from the heat and add the
baking chocolate and chocolate chips. Let the mixture sit
with the chocolate fully submerged for 2 minutes, and then
whisk until smooth. If the baking chocolate hasn't fully melted
after whisking, return the saucepan to the stove top and
heat over medium heat, whisking until the chocolate is fully
incorporated. Whisk in the vanilla.

Pour the chocolate mixture into a large bowl. Sift the
confectioners' sugar over the chocolate in three batches,
whisking after each addition. Place plastic wrap over the
frosting and refrigerate for about 40 minutes, or until thick
enough to frost the cake, stirring after 20 minutes and again
at the end of chilling. The frosting will be dense and firm.

If you prefer a lighter texture and color, whip the chilled
frosting in a stand mixer with the paddle attachment until
lightened. Use immediately after whipping, as the frosting
will firm up again if you allow it to sit.

Pastry Cream

MAKES 2 CUPS

2 cups whole milk or canned unsweetened
coconut milk (shake cans before opening)

1 teaspoon vanilla bean paste
(see page 196)

¼ teaspoon fine sea salt

3 tablespoons cornstarch

½ cup plus 2 teaspoons organic cane sugar

4 egg yolks

4 tablespoons unsalted butter or Earth
Balance Vegan Buttery Stick, at room
temperature

Combine the milk and vanilla bean paste in a heavy-bottomed
saucepan and bring to a boil over medium heat. While the milk
mixture heats (keep an eye on it so it doesn't boil over), whisk
together the salt, cornstarch, and sugar in a heatproof mixing
bowl (do not use aluminum). Add the egg yolks to the sugar
mixture and whisk until smooth.

When the milk mixture reaches the boiling point, add one-
fourth of the milk mixture to the egg mixture in the bowl,
whisking vigorously to combine. Quickly pour all the egg
mixture into the saucepan and return to medium heat. Bring
to a low boil (small bubbles, not a full rolling boil), whisking
constantly, and boil until the pastry cream thickens, about
2 minutes. Remove from the heat and immediately strain
through a fine-mesh strainer or sieve. Let cool for 10 minutes,
lightly stirring from time to time to help release the heat.

Cut the butter into 1-tablespoon pieces and add to the
pastry cream, one piece at a time, whisking each piece until
it dissolves before adding the next piece. Cover the pastry
cream with plastic wrap, pressing the wrap directly onto the
surface so it doesn't form a skin.

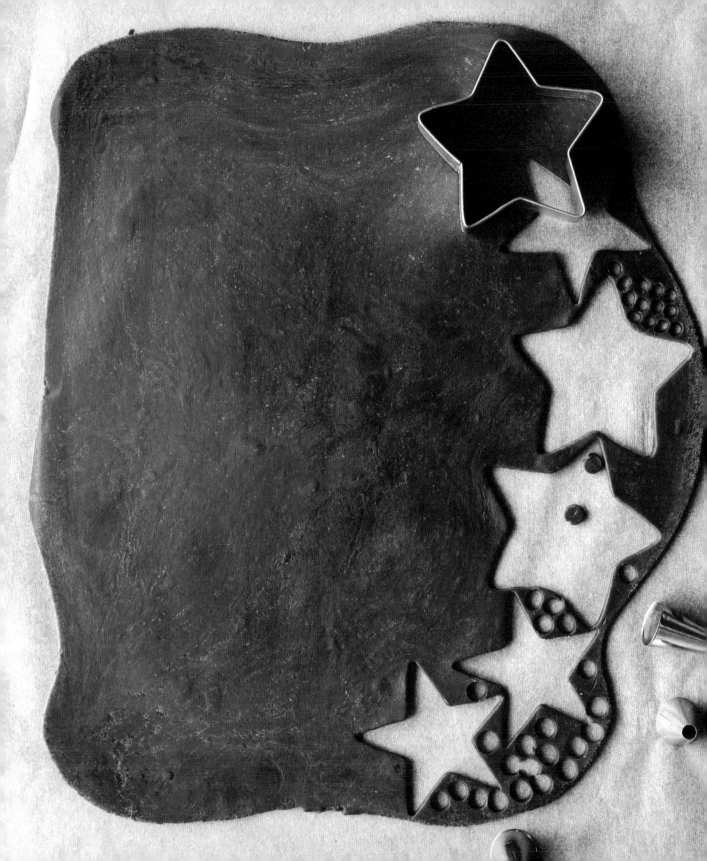

TIPS, TRICKS
& DECORATING
— *techniques* —

Beating the ingredients, slicing a cake into multiple layers, filling it with lemon curd, ganache, or fresh fruit, swirling or piping it with buttercream, and topping it with a beautiful garnish or chocolate decor—making a cake is such a joy! First, you need to know the basics, like how to measure ingredients, the best way to grease and line a pan, and trouble-free ways to remove cakes and cupcakes from their pans. Then it's on to essential decorating techniques, like filling and frosting cupcakes and layer cakes. The special decorating techniques section is where you'll learn how to execute piping techniques—from basic to over-the-top designs, gorgeous textured treatments, and other fancy touches that'll finish any cake in style, plus beautiful chocolate decor that'll make you feel like a tried-and-true pastry chef.

The key word here is fun. There's no such thing as a perfect cake, outside of special sugar art competitions where the cakes are made of Styrofoam. Whether the flaw is crumbs in your buttercream, uneven spatula strokes, or chaos caused by a kiddie's curious finger, there is a way to cover it up with garnishes, a dollop of whipped cream, or modeling chocolate. Whatever your solution, don't stress over tiny flaws. As we all know, an imperfect-looking cake tastes just as divine as a flawless one.

Mixing and Baking

Measuring Ingredients

For liquids, always use a clear glass or plastic measuring cup. To measure dry ingredients accurately, use the metal or plastic cups that come in nested sets. To measure flour accurately, scoop it into a standard dry measuring cup, and level the top of the flour by passing the back of a knife across to remove the excess flour. This technique will be important when you prepare the two gluten-free flour blends (page 191) used to make every cake in this book. And I hope it goes without mentioning that you should use measuring spoons to measure both liquid and dry ingredients—never tableware teaspoons and tablespoons!

Greasing Pans

If you're accustomed to using butter or shortening and flour to prepare your cake pans for baking, I'm here to tell you that you're wasting your time. Cooking spray and parchment paper are the best tools to keep from sticking, and they are far more affordable. Lightly spray the bottom and sides of your pan (hold the pan over the sink to avoid getting spray on the floor). Line it with parchment (place the pan on the paper, trace it, and cut out a circle just inside the line), and then spray again.

Gauging Oven Temperature

If you discover that your cakes are coming out underbaked or overbaked when you follow the cooking times in these recipes, your oven may not be properly calibrated. Pick up an oven thermometer and hang it on the center rack of your oven. Once you've set the oven temperature, allow 15 minutes for the oven to fully preheat, check your oven thermometer to confirm that you've reached the desired heat level, and if the temperature is higher or lower than desired, adjust the heat level on your oven setting accordingly.

Testing Cakes for Doneness

Testing a cake or cupcakes for doneness with a toothpick is the method I recommend for most of the cakes in this book. Simply insert a toothpick into the center of the cake. If the cake is done, the toothpick will come out clean, or perhaps with a few crumbs clinging to it. If there is uncooked batter or lots of damp crumbs on the toothpick, return the cake to the oven and set your timer for 5 to 10 minutes before retesting.

Removing a Cake from a Pan

Run a paring knife around the edge of the cake, between the cake and the edges of the pan. Place a wire cooling rack on top of the cake pan and invert the pan onto the rack, removing the pan to allow the cake to fall onto the rack. If the cake does not easily release from the pan, gently tap the pan against the counter to help release the cake. Place another rack on top of the cake and turn it over again so it's right-side up.

Removing Cupcakes from a Pan

To remove the cupcakes from the pan, run a paring knife around the edge of each cup. This should be necessary only if the batter rose up above the liner and ran over the edge onto the pan during baking. Turn the pan on its side and gently hit it on the counter to release the cupcakes.

Storing Cakes

When wrapping cake rounds, tightly wrap each one individually with plastic wrap; the plastic should be taut against the cake—no sags, no bags. The trick is to keep the plastic wrap attached to the roll and put the cake on top of the wrap, not underneath it (the wrap will never be airtight that way). Pull out a sheet of plastic large enough to wrap your cake layer and place the cake in the center of the sheet. Now you can tear off the piece of plastic and tightly wrap up your cake.

If you don't own an airtight container large enough to store your finished cake, you can loosely tent the cake with plastic wrap. Use multiple sheets of wrap to create a "bubble" around your cake, anchor the plastic wrap under the cake plate, and don't pull the plastic tightly down onto your cake. If your icing or decorations are tacky even when set (ganache, for example), you can use a few carefully placed toothpicks to lift the plastic off the surface of the cake. If the toothpicks leave holes, you can strategically place your garnish to cover them.

If you plan to freeze the cake, repeat with a second piece of plastic wrap. Plastic wrap sticks to plastic wrap, so for a successful seal, use more wrap than you think you need so it overlaps to create an airtight seal. If the seal isn't airtight, your cake won't taste fresh after thawing. Thaw at room temperature before removing the plastic and filling and frosting the cake.

Ready for Filling and Frosting

Coloring the Frosting

Whenever you can, work with gel food coloring (or other glycerine-based colors), never liquid colors, as gel colors are made to properly blend with fat-based ingredients like buttercream and chocolate. I like PME brand; they have a variety of 100 percent natural food colorings that deliver intense color in a wide range of hues.

Begin with enough buttercream to ice the top and sides of your cake or all of your cupcakes; it's difficult to re-create the exact shade, so you don't want to run out. Dip a toothpick into the gel of choice (or squeeze out a small drop), and swirl it into the icing. Add color a little at a time, using a new toothpick each time to avoid getting buttercream into your jar, until you achieve the desired shade. Note that colors will darken or intensify after an hour or two, so you may want to go a little lighter than your ultimate vision. When you like the color you see, blend the colored icing well with a rubber spatula.

Splitting Cake Layers

If you want to create a four-layer cake rather than a two-layer one, you'll need to split your cake layers in half horizontally. This isn't all that difficult to master, but you absolutely must use a proper serrated knife to create four clean, even layers.

Place one cake layer on your counter on a piece of parchment paper. Assuming you are right-handed, hold the knife in your right hand and place your left hand lightly on top of the cake layer. Place the knife blade horizontally against the side of the cake, right at the midpoint. Use your left hand to rotate the cake while applying pressure with the knife to gently score a mark all the way around the cake; don't cut all the way through yet, just cut about 1/4 inch into the cake. (Remember, you are rotating the cake and holding the knife fairly still, not sawing with the knife.) After you've marked a guideline, make a second pass, this time cutting into the cake about 2 inches deep all the way around, using the scoring mark as your guide. Then make one final pass, this time pulling the knife all the way into the center of the cake to cut the cake in half. Now you have two layers. Slide them onto a sheet of parchment paper or a baking sheet and set aside. Repeat the process with your second layer of cake.

Filling and Frosting Layer Cakes

The key to successful filling and frosting is to avoid spreading rogue crumbs everywhere. Here's how: always keep your offset spatula or knife on the filling or icing and *never* touch the cake directly with the tool you're using. You want to use your spatula to push and spread the filling or icing, using more than you think you need to avoid touching the cake directly. Be gentle, working slowly until you develop a rhythm. If you are making a four-layer cake, you'll be working with layers that have a cut surface. This cut surface is particularly prone to getting crumby, so use extra caution.

Before you begin, make sure your filling or icing is at room temperature. You *cannot* properly fill or frost a cake with cold buttercream or ganache. If you made your buttercream ahead and refrigerated it, bring it to room temperature and beat in the bowl of a stand mixer to restore its proper texture and volume. If you're picking up crumbs, give the cake a rest in the refrigerator for 30 minutes or so. The cold cake will be firmer and less likely to release crumbs.

To fill a two-layer cake, place one cake layer on a serving platter. Scoop some buttercream or ganache onto the cake and, using an offset spatula, butter knife, or the back of a spoon, smooth out the icing to create a nice even layer on the top. Top with the second cake layer, upside down so that the top of the cake will be flat and pressing down firmly. Finally, frost the sides of the cake.

To fill a four-layer cake, scoop some buttercream or ganache onto the first layer of the cake and, using an offset spatula, butter knife, or the back of a spoon, smooth out the icing to create a nice even layer on the top. Top with the second cake layer, cut side down, press down firmly, and repeat the frosting application. Repeat with the remaining two cake layers and frosting, making sure your top layer is applied upside down so that the top of the cake is flat. Finally, frost the sides of the cake. If you have time, chill your filled cake in the refrigerator until firm, about 1 hour, before applying the icing to the sides and top.

Always start with the top and then move to the sides. Drop some frosting in the top center of the cake and spread it to the edges. You're not trying to create a perfect surface at this point; you just want to get the top of the cake covered with a fairly even layer.

Now move to the sides. Scoop some frosting onto your spatula and spread it on the side of the cake. Continue with additional scoops until you have covered the sides, all the way down to the bottom edge of the cake, right against your plate or platter.

If you want to finish the surface of your buttercream with old-fashioned swoops and swirls, see page 180 for instructions. There, you'll find other impressive ways to texture the buttercream, including vertical or horizontal stripes or a smooth-as-glass mirror finish.

Frosting Cupcakes

Before you begin, make sure your buttercream or ganache is at room temperature. If you made the buttercream ahead and refrigerated it, beat in the bowl of a stand mixer to restore its proper texture before applying it to the cupcakes. (A ganache will not need beating before using.)

For a simple, home-style icing treatment, use an offset spatula or butter knife. Place a couple tablespoons of buttercream or ganache on top of the cupcake, and spread it to cover the top of the cupcake all the way to the edges of the paper cup. You can use your spatula or knife or even the back of a spoon to make swirls in the icing, if you like. If you're inclined to use a pastry bag, a round or star tip is best for piping cupcakes. For lots of creative ideas for piping frosting onto cupcakes, from swirls, to spikes, to a round cupcake mound, see the techniques described on pages 175 to 180.

If you're applying garnish or decoration to the cupcakes, do so before the buttercream or ganache has had time to form a crust, usually within about 20 minutes of applying the frosting, to ensure that your garnish will stick.

Making and Filling Holes in Cupcakes

In addition to icing for the tops of the cupcakes, many of my cupcake recipes include a surprise filling. Using a paring knife, remove the centers of the cupcakes: insert the knife into the top of a cupcake at a 45-degree angle, about halfway between the center and edge of the cupcake, and then cut all the way around, creating a hole about 1 inch deep and 1 inch wide. Repeat with the remaining cupcakes. Reserve the pieces of cake you remove for snacking, or layer them in a dish with whipped cream and fresh fruit to make a simple trifle. To fill the holes with the filling called for in the recipe, simply spoon it in. The holes will be covered up by the frosting.

Slicing a Cake

Cake should be served at room temperature for best flavor. Use a warm, dry knife for the cleanest slices. Run the knife under hot tap water and wipe it dry between each cut. Any sharp, thin-bladed knife will do the job, just be sure to wipe the blade clean between cuts.

Decorating Cakes

Piping Techniques

While you certainly don't have to become a full-on cake artist to decorate the cakes and cupcakes in this book, in this section I share some piping techniques—from simple to fancy—that you can play with. You can use these techniques to pipe buttercream, cooled ganache, or whipped cream. Buttercream is the most versatile, and easiest, to work with. Buttercream should be piped at cool room temperature, ganache at cool room temperature or slightly chilled, and whipped cream must always be very cold and piped just prior to serving. To properly execute these piping techniques, you will need to purchase some basic equipment if you don't already own it: piping bags, tips, and two-part couplers (see page 198).

Insert the cone-shaped part of a coupler into the bottom of a pastry bag so that the first two or three threads peek through the hole. (Trim the bag with scissors if necessary to make the cone fit properly.) Now slip your chosen tip over the smooth end of the cone and attach the ring, screwing it firmly into place.

If you're right-handed, make a C with your left hand and fingers and turn your wrist so that the C is parallel to the floor (if you're left-handed, reverse these instructions). Place the bag in the C with the tip end pointing to the floor and fold the open end of the bag down over your hand to create a cuff. Using a rubber spatula, large spoon, or offset spatula, with your right hand, scoop the frosting into the bottom of the bag. Close the C around the spatula before you pull it out of the bag to scrape all of the frosting cleanly into the bag. Open your hand and insert more frosting, taking care not to overfill the bag: one-third to one-half full is ideal.

With the tip held over the bowl of frosting, close off the open end of the bag with your fingertips and shake the frosting down vigorously to eliminate air pockets and encourage the frosting to collect at the tip end. With the curved area between your right thumb and forefinger, squeeze the bag above the bulge of frosting and twist it tightly counterclockwise to close the bag, using the thumb and base knuckle on the forefinger of your right hand to pinch the back closed. (If you need to set the bag aside, make sure it is twisted tightly, and then fold the excess material over the bulge and set the bag, bulge side down, in a bowl or large glass. The tip end should be pointing up, so the bag stays sealed and the frosting doesn't seep out.)

You'll use both hands when piping. Using your right hand (or left if that's your dominant hand), hold the bag firmly closed and apply pressure to dispense the icing. Wrap your palm and other fingers around the bulge of frosting in the bag. You'll use these fingers to apply pressure as you create your designs.

Regardless of the design you're making, there will always be certain constants: you will squeeze and then release pressure on the bag to dispense the frosting and create the design. Playing around with this squeeze-and-release rhythm on a piece of parchment paper is a great way to practice and get a feel for the equipment. You can scoop up the piped frosting and put it back in the bag to reuse.

ROUND OR PLAIN TIP DESIGNS

Dots Single dots and the triple "Swiss" dot (see page 178) can be used in endless variations on cakes and cupcakes. Hold the bag vertically just above the cake or cupcake. Apply pressure to dispense the frosting—a little pressure for a small dot and more pressure for a larger dot. Release the pressure first, and then quickly pull the bag up and away from the dot. If you have a little "tail" on the top of your dot, simply use a lightly dampened fingertip to press the tail down; this will smooth out the top of your dot and make it more professional looking.

Star

Petal

Leaf

Petal

Star

Petal

Star

Writing on cakes Use round tips for writing on cakes. Writing takes practice, so roll out some parchment paper over some text you've written with a pen, and trace the text with your icing. Try holding the bag at different angles to see what feels natural for you; most people are more comfortable with the bag in a more vertical position. You'll have to apply pressure for the entire letter or series of letters if doing cursive, so plan ahead and look for places where you can stop to rest your hand. For example, when piping "Congratulations," I connect the C-o-n-g-r-a-t, stop to twist and tighten the bag, and then continue with the u-l-a-t-i-o-n-s. When just learning to pipe on cakes you can "cheat" by lightly tracing the text into the cake icing with the tip of a toothpick and then pipe over the tracing.

Round tip borders for cakes Round tips can also be used to create a variety of borders. The two most common are called connecting pearl and snail trail (see page 178). Connecting pearl is a row of individually piped dots or "pearls" placed right against one another. Simply repeat the dot technique described above, placing the dots directly next to one another. Snail trail is a true border in that the design flows in one motion from start to finish. Hold the bag at a 45-degree angle. Squeeze the dot to the size you want, and then stop squeezing and pull the tip away to create a tail; without lifting the tip away from the cake, squeeze again to create another dot atop the tail, and then stop squeezing and pull away again. Continue this squeeze-and-pull rhythm all the way around the top edge or base of your cake. You can vary the size of your borders considerably by simply varying the amount and duration of pressure you apply.

Round cupcake mound A beautifully rounded mound of icing atop a cupcake is perfection at its simplest, as you can see on the Banana Cream Cupcakes (page 74). It's the ideal base for additional decorations, such as dipped berries or banana chips. You don't even need a tip to make this one. The coupler cone (with no tip attached) is the perfect shape and size for achieving this finish. Hold the bag vertically and about ½ inch above the center of your cupcake. Apply even pressure to the bag to dispense the frosting, and while slowly drawing the bag away from the cupcake,

continue pressing until the frosting puddles out almost to the edge of the cupcake. When you have the mound you want, stop applying pressure and quickly pull away the tip, straight up to get that little spike.

Round cupcake swirl Use the coupler without a tip attached. Hold the bag vertically and place the tip at the edge of the cupcake. Apply even pressure as you swirl the tip around toward the center in a spiral motion, starting with a larger circle and ending with a tiny circle, until you've covered the top of the cupcake. You can keep the swirl low or build the design up high, depending on the look you want to achieve.

Petal Icing for Cakes This beautiful effect adds lots of texture to your cakes; see the Chocolate Peppermint Cake (page 64). Use the coupler cone to pipe a vertical row of 1-inch-diameter beads up the side of the cake. Using an offset spatula or the back of a spoon held horizontally, press down into the bottom bead then pull and drag the icing to the right to create a petal shape. Repeat the process with the other beads in the first vertical row. Now pipe a second vertical row about ¾ inch to the right of the first, overlapping the dragged icing, and repeat the dragging process. Add more vertical rows all the way around the side of your cake until the cake sides are completely covered with rows of petals.

STAR TIP DESIGNS

Star and rosette The star is one of the easiest piping designs. Holding the bag vertically, use the same squeeze-and-release technique described on page 175 for the dot to create individual stars. To create rosettes, swirl the tip in a counterclockwise motion while applying pressure. Begin in the center of where you want your rosette to end up, and swirl around this point. (See examples on page 181.)

Star tip borders for cakes Star tips can be used to create many borders, both simple and intricate. Two favorites are shell and zigzag (see page 181). The shell is similar to the snail trail made using the round tip (see above); it's essentially the same motion, using the squeeze-and-pull rhythm, but when you're using a star tip, you end up with

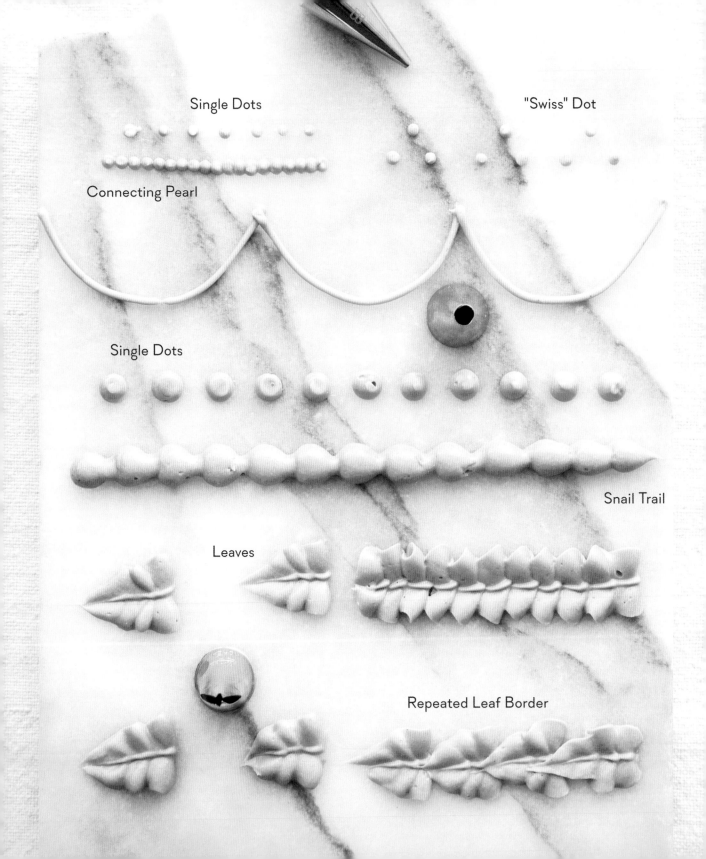

Single Dots

"Swiss" Dot

Connecting Pearl

Single Dots

Snail Trail

Leaves

Repeated Leaf Border

Star spikes Using any small star tip, cover the top surface of your cupcake or cake with spiky stars. Emphasize the tail of the star by pulling the tip away from the surface of the cake before you stop applying pressure; this creates a taller, more dramatic "spike" rather than a flat star. See examples on pages 60 and 181.

Star cupcake swirl Using the large star tip (number 1B), make the same motion as described in the round cupcake swirl technique on page 177. To create a tall swirl, make two or three circular passes to build up the icing; see the cupcakes on page 84. Or to create a swirl that resembles a rose, make just one swirl, directly on the cupcake surface. Starting at the center and swirling to the outside of the cupcake will give a slightly different effect from starting at the edges. Try both and see which you prefer.

LEAF TIP DESIGNS

The leaf tip, as the name suggests, is designed to create leaf-shape frosting decorations. It also makes lovely borders when the leaf motif is repeated around a cake's base or top edge. Practice is essential for success with the leaf tip, as you must cultivate just the right amount of pressure on the bag combined with the perfect pulling motion to elongate and thin the tip of the leaf. (Practice this one on parchment paper before piping on a cake or cupcake.)

Leaves To make a leaf, snug the tip right where you want the base of the leaf to begin. Apply pressure to dispense the icing and slowly pull the tip away to form the leaf, and then stop applying pressure as you quickly pull away to thin and elongate the end of the leaf.

Leaf border for cakes Repeat the leaf shape described above, overlapping the leaves slightly, to create a border. Make your border straight, or alternate the angles of your leaves to create a zigzag effect.

a row of little shells. For zigzag, apply an even pressure on the bag to dispense the frosting while moving the tip back and forth in a zigzag motion. You can keep the pattern even or vary it by combining short zigzags with wider zigzags. Play around and have fun with it.

Star rosettes to cover a cake Using the large star tip (number 1B), you can create a beautiful rose-covered cake in just a few minutes by piping rows of swirls around the sides and the top of the cake. Start with a thinly iced cake. Begin at the bottom of the cake. Hold your bag horizontally, with the tip just off the surface of the cake, about 1 inch up the side. Pipe a large rosette against the side of the cake. Pipe another rosette right next to the first and continue all the way around the cake. Pipe a second row above the first, placing the rosettes offset from the first row. Depending on the height of your cake, you may need a third row. If desired, you can pipe rosettes to cover the top of your cake also; see the Hummingbird Cake (page 47).

PETAL TIP DESIGNS

Ruffled ribbon icing for cakes Petal tips can be curved, straight, or U-shaped. I use the straight tip (#104) to create a ruffled ribbon icing on cakes. The tip has an opening that is wider on one end. Hold the bag vertically with the tip at the base of the cake, with the wider end of the tip positioned toward the side of the cake. Apply pressure while moving the tip in a quick back-and-forth motion (about 1 inch wide), raising the tip to stack the ribbon icing on top of itself up the side of the cake. Continue this technique around the sides of cake, and on top of the cake, too, if desired (see right).

Textured Treatments

You don't need a piping bag to create these special effects on the surface of buttercream-frosted cakes. A butter knife or an offset spatula and a spoon are the only tools required.

SWOOPS AND SWIRLS

Grab a spoon to create these easy effects reminiscent of old-fashioned, home-baked cakes. Starting on the top of a freshly iced cake and then moving to the sides, press the back of the spoon lightly into the frosting, and then pull away to create a swoop effect. For swirls, press the back of the spoon into the icing, and then swirl it in a figure-eight shape before pulling the spoon away. If you don't like the results, simply smooth out the frosting with a spatula or knife, and then give it another go with the back of the spoon. For an example, see the Very Vanilla Cake on page 40.

VERTICAL STRIPES

Start with a freshly frosted cake; be sure to smooth out the frosting evenly so you have a clean surface to work with. You'll use a small offset spatula or a butter knife, held horizontally, and start at the base of the cake. Lightly press the end of the spatula into the icing at the base of the cake and drag it up the side of the cake to the top edge, and then back down to the base while turning the cake slowly so that you zig and zag up and down the full height of the cake all the way around. You can stop after a few strokes to check the effect; if you're not satisfied, just smooth out the frosting and start again. Try applying

different amounts of pressure and varying the width of your zigzag for different effects. If it's easier for you, put the cake on a turntable (a.k.a. lazy Susan). It allows you to concentrate on your stripes, and makes the process more effortless.

HORIZONTAL STRIPES

A turntable and an offset spatula are absolutely necessary to create this finish. Place your freshly frosted cake on the turntable. Hold the offset spatula (small spatula for thin stripes, large spatula for wide stripes) horizontally at the base of your cake. Lightly press the spatula into the icing and use your other hand to smoothly rotate the turntable, keeping the pressure on the spatula. When you have completed one rotation (and one horizontal stripe), move the spatula up above the first stripe (do not release your pressure on the spatula when you make this adjustment). Continue to rotate the turntable and press on the spatula until you have created stripes all the way to the top edge of the cake. You can stripe the top of the cake in the same manner, creating circles that start at the outer edge and swirl inward to the center. Press your spatula into the

Individual Stars

Rosettes

Zigzag

Star Spikes

Rosettes

icing on the outer edge of the top of the cake and rotate the turntable, applying even pressure from outer edge to center. (Don't lift the spatula during this process.)

MIRROR FINISH

There's nothing more professional looking than tiers of perfectly smooth buttercream-iced cake. To achieve this look, you will need a turntable, a bench scraper with sharp (not rounded) corners, hot water, and a lint-free kitchen rag or paper towels. I like to work close to hot running water, but if that's not convenient for you, you can just keep a large pan of hot water next to you while you work. Start with a freshly (and generously) frosted cake.

Hold the bench scraper under the hot tap water (or set it in your pan of hot water) until the blade is very warm to the touch. Wipe the blade completely dry with the rag or paper towels and position the blade vertically against the side of the cake. Press the blade into the frosting while turning the cake away from you slowly. Hold the blade still while rotating the turntable; if you move it you won't achieve the perfect mirror finish you're aiming for. The heat from the blade will subtly melt the icing as your blade passes over it.

Don't worry: you don't have to go all the way around the cake in one motion. Cover as much territory as you can comfortably, and then stop and wipe any icing off the blade, rinse it under hot water to reheat, wipe dry, and go at it again, picking up where you left off. For the smoothest finish, you'll want to make several passes around the sides of the cake with the warm, dry blade. Excess icing is likely to accumulate at the top edge of the cake. Use your offset spatula to spread the icing toward the center of the cake top to create a clean top edge. To further smooth the top of the cake, run your offset spatula under hot water and wipe it dry. Hold the spatula horizontally, with the blade at a 45-degree angle, and stroke from the outer edge to the center. Work in small sections all the way around the cake, stopping to reheat your spatula blade as necessary.

Chocolate Decor

Cake artists refer to the decorations applied to the tops and sides of an iced cake as decor. Decor is the extra bling that makes your cake really shine.

CHOCOLATE SHAVINGS

You can use any number of kitchen tools to create chocolate shavings of varying sizes: a box grater, vegetable peeler, paring knife, melon ball scoop (my favorite), or small round cookie cutter. Use a block or large bar of chocolate, at least 4 ounces in weight, so you have something to really grab on to while you're shaving it. Hold the block of chocolate with a paper towel over a baking sheet lined with parchment paper. Grate, peel, or scrape the shavings directly onto the lined pan, trying not to touch the shavings with your bare hands, as they will melt quickly. See page 118 for an example.

The temperature and type of chocolate will determine the texture and quality of your shavings. If the chocolate is dry and crumbly, you'll need to warm the chocolate slightly by rubbing the surface with the palm of your hand. If your kitchen is very warm, the chocolate may be too soft (especially if you're working with white chocolate); in this case, refrigerate the chocolate for 2 to 5 minutes to firm it up. Dark chocolate is firmer and harder at room temperature than milk or white chocolate. Milk chocolate is the easiest to work with for shaving; it's neither too hard nor too soft. Shavings can be stored in an airtight container in the fridge indefinitely.

Finishes for Cake Tops

STENCILS

You can purchase stencils in hundreds of patterns at hobby shops or cut your own from parchment paper or acetate, in designs ranging from hearts and simple flowers to monograms and animals. Allow your frosted cake to set at room temperature for about 1 hour to form a crust. Simply lay the stencil on top of the cake and, using a fine-mesh sieve or flour sifter, lightly sift cocoa powder, confectioners' sugar, or cinnamon over the stencil until the negative spaces are filled. Lift the stencil straight up and away from the cake so as not to mar the finish.

DRIZZLING GANACHE

Your ganache must be warm and semiliquid to drizzle properly, so heat it in the microwave at half power for 10 seconds at a time, or in the top of a simmering double boiler, if necessary. You don't want it piping hot, just warm enough so it is easy to drizzle onto the top of the cake.

Place about $\frac{1}{4}$ cup of the warm ganache in a small resealable plastic bag and seal the bag. Snip one corner to create a $\frac{1}{16}$-inch-diameter hole. (When in doubt start with a smaller hole than you think you might need; you can always enlarge it with a second cut, if necessary.) Hold the bag over the cake with the hole facing up so the ganache doesn't drip out. Turn the bag over so the hole faces down and immediately begin moving your hand in a zigzag motion over the top of the cake. (If you're nervous about this step, you can practice over a piece of parchment paper before you try zigzagging the ganache onto the cake.)

Depending on the consistency of your ganache, you may need to apply light pressure to the bag to get the ganache moving. The drizzle should be random and freeform; there's no right or wrong way for it to look. You can zigzag in just one direction or crisscross the top of the cake. You can create a light pattern with just a few passes of your hand or go crazy and layer the ganache more heavily.

GANACHE EDGE DRIP

This is a lovely technique to use on cakes frosted with white or chocolate buttercream. Using ganache in a semiliquid state, fill a disposable plastic piping bag and snip a large hole about the diameter of a pencil eraser. Pipe the ganache slowly along the top edge of the iced cake so that it drips down the sides. Allow the ganache to set at room temperature for at least 30 minutes or up to 1 day before serving.

Chocolate Modeling Paste Decor

Chocolate modeling paste is a versatile (and delicious) medium for creating a multitude of cake and cupcake decorations ranging from cutouts and confetti to hand-modeled figures and wrapped cake tiers.

Chocolate Modeling Paste

Using high-quality chocolate for your modeling paste will give you the best flavor and handling results. Extra modeling chocolate can be kept at cool room temperature for up to 2 months. Wrap it tightly in plastic wrap and store in a resealable plastic bag.

2⅔ cups dark chocolate chips
6 to 8 tablespoons pure honey or light agave syrup

Prepare a double boiler by adding 1 inch of water to a small saucepan and topping it with a stainless steel bowl that fits comfortably atop the pan without the bottom touching the water. Bring the water to a simmer. Place the chocolate chips in the bowl and let them melt slowly. If the water starts to boil rapidly, remove the entire double boiler from the heat or reduce the heat so the water returns to a simmer. Gently stir the chocolate with a rubber spatula now and then, but do not overwork the chocolate.

When the chocolate has melted, remove the bowl from the pan and wipe the bottom dry. Place the bowl on the counter and let cool about 5 minutes, or until the chocolate is warm to the touch. Pour 6 tablespoons of the honey into the chocolate and stir with a spatula to combine. If the chocolate thickens or seizes (becomes clumpy), continue to stir vigorously until the honey is fully incorporated. If the mixture does not come together completely, stir in up to 2 tablespoons additional honey.

The chocolate mixture should be thick, like a dough, and it may be a bit sticky at this point. If the mixture is very sticky, place it on a piece of parchment paper and allow it to air-dry for 30 minutes. Transfer the modeling paste to a resealable plastic bag and seal the bag. Let rest for at least 1 hour or overnight.

VARIATION: White Chocolate Modeling Paste

Prepare according to the directions above, but substitute white chocolate chips for the dark chocolate chips.

WRAPPED TIERS (ROUND OR SQUARE)

Wrapping your cake tier in modeling chocolate has an effect similar to fondant, but tastes infinitely better. Start with a smoothly frosted, very well-chilled buttercream cake. To get a good estimate of how large a sheet of modeling paste you'll need to wrap your cake, measure across the top of your cake with a measuring tape, and then measure the height of the cake. Multiply the height by two and add the measurement across the top plus 2 inches for a buffer. (For example, an 8-inch-diameter cake that is 4 inches tall will require a piece of paste that's 18 inches in diameter.) It's better to roll out a larger piece of paste than you think you'll need rather than come up short. See pages 128 and 134 for examples.

Once you know approximately what size you need, roll out the paste on a lightly oiled countertop to $\frac{1}{4}$ inch thick, rolling the paste evenly and smoothly and stopping occasionally to check that the paste is not sticking to your counter. Add more oil to the counter if needed. When your sheet of paste reaches the desired size, bring your cake to the counter, next to the sheet. Slide your hands, palms facing up, under the paste, and using soft palms and straight fingers, lift the paste up and over the cake. Center the paste on top of the cake. Beginning with the top of the cake, smooth out any air bubbles, and then gently smooth the paste onto the sides of the cake, working from the top down and removing any air bubbles as you go, all the way down to the bottom edge of the cake. (Use soft hands, your palms primarily, and if you have long nails, keep your fingers flexed out so that your nails don't poke into the paste.) Once the paste is wrapped around the cake, use your palms to gently buff the paste smooth. Any trapped air bubbles can be pricked with a straight pin. Use a paring knife or pizza cutter to trim excess paste from the bottom edge of the cake. Repeat with any remaining cake tiers.

CUTOUTS

Roll out chocolate modeling paste into $\frac{1}{8}$-inch-thick sheets and use cookie cutters to create shapes such as hearts, diamonds, and flowers. Small shapes are perfect for topping cupcakes or placing around the sides of frosted cakes; larger shapes can be centered on a cake top. Try layering your cutouts for more visual interest; flowers are particularly well suited to this effect. You might cut two flowers and stack them with the petals offset. Or place a flower atop two cut-out leaves. Letters and numbers can also be cut out of modeling paste to form messages.

CONFETTI AND STREAMERS

Roll out the chocolate modeling paste into $\frac{1}{8}$-inch-thick sheets (see page 168). Cut tiny circles from several colors of modeling chocolate to create confetti. A round piping tip makes the perfect size. Sprinkle the confetti on top of cakes and cupcakes, around the base of a cake, or on serving plates. Create streamers by cutting $\frac{1}{4}$-inch-wide ribbon from the modeling chocolate, and then twist the ribbon to create a streamer and apply it casually, as if tossed, on top of a cake or around the bottom edge, on serving plates, or around a cake pedestal for a centerpiece cake.

Give It a Blast

My absolute favorite kitchen gadget is my blowtorch. Truth be told, it's not one of those cute culinary torches from Williams-Sonoma. No, mine is a full-on propane torch from the hardware store. Try toasting the tops of Lemon Meringue Cupcakes (page 92), S'mores Cakes (page 108), or Baked Alaska Bombes (page 103).

Whether you purchase it from a kitchen or hardware store, a torch is easy to use and, once you get one in your hands, you may want to use it every chance you get. Torches vary in their power, so you'll need to experiment with yours to get the feel for how long it takes to achieve various levels of browning. Start with a lower flame.

Apply the tip of the flame to the area you want to torch. Start with a quick pass over the area you're browning to see whether you get any result, and then repeat until you get the toasty golden brown effect you're looking for. I like to focus a little extra heat (and browning) on the tips and peaks. If your meringue or marshmallow catches fire, don't panic—just pull away the torch and blow out the flame.

It's obvious, but I have to say it: when using a blowtorch, you're working with an exposed flame, so you need to pay full attention to what you're doing and be aware of your surroundings. Don't fire up your torch when young children are around. This is not the time to wear a scarf or drapy sleeves, and if you have very long hair, pull it back.

YOUR GLUTEN-FREE BAKING PANTRY

Ingredients

If you want to bake a fabulous gluten-free cake, then you need to use high-quality ingredients. It pays off in so many ways! I recommend baking with organic ingredients (see page 190), but don't worry, if going completely organic is not practical for you, in this section I help you prioritize by pointing out key ingredients where organic is especially important—and explain why. Remember, cake is a sometimes food, so choose the best ingredients you can find and enjoy the occasional indulgence. The Sources on page 204 tell you where you can buy them.

Know Your Ingredients

This book is all about creating luscious cakes *everyone* can enjoy, so it's important to know that the building blocks of your creations—the ingredients—fit your dietary needs and will make for the most delicious results possible. Here are some recommendations to help you select the best ingredients at the grocery store.

Gluten Free To make sure the cakes you're baking are completely gluten free, you'll need to use my gluten-free flour blends (page 191) and carefully select your leaveners and thickeners (especially baking powder and cornstarch), flavorings and food colorings, and even chocolate, all of which may contain hidden gluten. I've pointed out potential hazards and provided gluten-free brand recommendations throughout the book, along with the list of sources on page 204, which tells you where to buy them.

Never make assumptions about your ingredients. Check labels carefully for gluten or gluten-containing ingredients, and if the package information isn't clear, visit the company's website. *Note:* All the ingredients recommended in this book are 100 percent gluten free. But occasionally, companies change their formulations, adding gluten to their products (boo!). If you're unsure about a particular product, check the gluten-free product watch lists found online.

Allergen Free Many of us following a gluten-free diet are also eliminating other allergens (or potential allergens) from our diets, such as dairy, eggs, soy, and nuts. I've made every effort to include alternative ingredients in my cake recipes so everyone can enjoy them. My Flax Egg Replacer (page 194) makes it easy to "veganize" many of my cakes, as do Earth Balance Vegan Buttery Sticks (see page 193). And because nut allergies and sensitivities are so pervasive, I've included many nut-free cakes; the nuts can also be eliminated from a recipe if they are not a key ingredient in the cake.

I am not a fan of soy products: most of the soy produced in the United States is genetically modified and highly contaminated with pesticides. Overexposure to this low-quality soy can lead to soy sensitivities and allergies. The only soy product I suggest using is nondairy cream cheese for a dairy-free version of cream cheese frosting. Alternatively, you can substitute one of my buttercreams, preparing it with vegetable shortening as directed.

To see which recipes meet your dietary requirements, you can consult the Allergen-Free and Vegan Cakes Chart on page 200.

Organic When baking, I recommend that you use organic dairy products (milk, butter, and yogurt) and pasture-raised eggs (see page 194). Organic dairy is not only free of GMOs, pesticides, hormones, and antibiotics, but it's also higher in nutritive value and simply tastes better. I also recommend that you use whole-fat dairy (or dairy-free substitutions like coconut milk) in your baking, not reduced-fat or skim versions. Fat is not the enemy—it contributes flavor and superior texture to baked goods.

I also suggest that you use organic, minimally processed sweeteners (cane sugar, coconut palm sugar, honey, and maple syrup). In my cakes, I choose chocolate that is gluten, dairy, and soy free and high in cacao for great flavor; for details, see page 194. I also opt for organic spices; for an excellent source, see Frontier, page 206.

Natural The idea of an "unnatural" food would have been bizarre to our ancestors, but today fake foods containing all sorts of chemical additives, preservatives, and artificial colors and flavorings abound. Artificial colors are particularly notorious, causing a laundry list of symptoms in sensitive individuals and increasing the risk of cancer. I use Rumford aluminum-free baking powder exclusively (see page 197). Aluminum has no place in our food or in our bodies; it has been linked to increased incidence of Alzheimer's disease, cancer, and infertility. Instead, use the all-natural ingredients I recommend below (including natural flavorings and fruit spreads).

Gluten-Free Flour

Making the switch to gluten-free cake baking is not just a simple matter of swapping one flour for another. You need to come up with a flour blend that re-creates the same flavor and texture in your cakes, as well as the binding, structure, and elasticity that gluten provides. So you also need to use a binder, like xanthan gum (see page 197), to replace the gluten in conventional flour. Xanthan gum is crucial to successful gluten-free baking: it helps air pockets develop in your cakes and provides elasticity. Without it, your cakes will be very dense and heavy.

I've taken the guesswork out of this process: just mix up my two gluten-free flour blends (see opposite) and you'll be ready to go whenever you want to bake a cake. The result is cakes with the very best taste and texture—in fact, you'll be amazed at how closely they resemble cakes with gluten. These days, you can find the components in the gluten-free section of many supermarkets; if not, order from the sources provided on page 204. Depending on which cakes you're making, each batch of flour blend will make two or three cakes. If you bake often, make a double or triple batch of each blend and store them in the fridge for up to six months or in the freezer for up to one year.

Many gluten-free flour blends on the market contain baking soda, baking powder, or xanthan gum, so I would not recommend swapping most of them for my homemade flour blends. Although the recipes in this book were developed using my own flour blends, two gluten-free flour blends I like are Cup4Cup and Mama's Almond Blend gluten-free flour. Cup4Cup is free of baking soda and powder, but it does contain some xanthan gum. So if you were to swap it into one of my recipes that calls for xanthan gum, you should omit or decrease the amount of xanthan gum you use—otherwise, the cake may rise too much and then fall flat. For those who are dairy-free or vegan, note that Cup4Cup does contain some milk powder so Mama's would be a better option for you. Mama's Almond Blend gluten-free flour does not contain any leaveners, which makes it a good candidate for substitutions in a pinch; however, it does include almond meal, so it will be off-limits to some.

Gluten-Free All-Purpose Flour Blend

I use this blend whenever I would typically use all-purpose flour—only this one is 100 percent gluten free! For the best flavor and texture, I use Arrowhead Mills organic rice flour and tapioca and all-natural potato starch from Bob's Red Mill.

2 cups white rice flour
1 cup tapioca starch (also called tapioca flour)
1 cup potato starch (not flour)

In a large bowl, whisk the rice flour with the tapioca and potato starches until well combined. Store in an airtight container in your pantry or another cool, dark place up to 1 month.

For longer-term storage, keep in the refrigerator up to 6 months or in the freezer up to 1 year. Before using, bring to room temperature. Just before measuring, whisk the flour blend to aerate it in case it has settled. Sifting is not necessary if you whisk.

Gluten-Free Whole Grain Flour Blend

The feature of this whole grain blend is sorghum flour. Sorghum is an ancient grain; it adds protein and fiber, and its subtle flavor does not throw off the balance in sweet baked goods the way many other whole grain flours do. I use sorghum flour and all-natural potato starch from Bob's Red Mill and organic rice flour from Arrowhead Mills.

2 cups sweet sorghum flour
1 cup white rice flour
1 cup potato starch (not flour)

In a large bowl, whisk the sorghum flour, rice flour, and potato starch until well combined. Store in an airtight container in your pantry or another cool, dark place up to 1 month.

For longer-term storage, keep in the refrigerator up to 6 months or in the freezer up to 1 year. Before using, bring to room temperature. Just before measuring, whisk the flour blend to aerate it in case it has settled. Sifting is not necessary if you whisk.

Sweeteners

I use only unrefined organic sweeteners to replace the more customary hyperrefined white, brown, and confectioners' sugars, which are processed with bleaching agents, chemicals, or bone char. Unrefined sugars retain their nutritive and mineral value, and the organic label means that the sugarcane (or coconut) was grown without herbicides or pesticides. I call for organic cane sugar in the recipes because it is readily available and relatively affordable, but coconut palm sugar is my first choice for baking (see below). I also use natural unrefined sweeteners like honey and maple syrup to sweeten my coffee cakes and glazes.

Cane Sugar I use Wholesome Sweeteners brand exclusively (see page 206). Not only is it an unrefined, organic, fair-trade, non-GMO, vegan sugar, it's also hand-harvested and sustainably grown. The cane juice is squeezed from fresh sugarcane, evaporated, and crystallized to create a blond-colored sugar.

Brown Sugar I also use Wholesome Sweeteners brown sugar, which is based on the unrefined cane sugar described above with a little added molasses. Like refined brown sugar, it lends a deeper flavor and added moistness to baked goods—but it's more health supportive.

Coconut Palm Sugar This is a low-glycemic and more nutritive alternative that can be substituted for the organic cane sugar in all my recipes. Derived from the coconut tree, it has a pleasing, caramel-like flavor and dissolves in both hot and cold liquids. Navitas Naturals is my brand of choice; Wholesome Sweeteners is another good option.

Confectioners' Sugar Powdered sugar is another name for this finely ground sugar and also an apt description of its fine texture, which allows it to "melt" imperceptibly into other ingredients such as buttercreams and glazes. Wholesome Sweeteners brand is made from organic cane sugar that uses tapioca starch rather than genetically modified cornstarch to keep the sugar from caking. You can also make your own all-natural confectioners' sugar (see sidebar).

MAKE YOUR OWN CONFECTIONERS' SUGAR

Place organic cane sugar or coconut palm sugar in the bowl of a food processor with the blade attachment and process on high until very fine and powdery. (You may need to cover your feed tube with a towel to avoid getting a sugar fog facial.) Store the confectioners' sugar in an airtight container in your pantry and use in place of conventional powdered sugar. This homemade version will not be as fine and powdery, but for the purpose of glazing a cake it will work beautifully. You can store it in an airtight container at room temperature up to 3 months.

Maple Syrup One of the most used natural sweeteners, maple syrup is graded according to color and flavor. There are three Grade A's (light, medium, and dark) and one Grade B, which is darker even than the Grade A dark. The darker the maple syrup, the more intense the flavor and the higher the nutritive value (assuming you're using *real* maple syrup). The differences are the result of the time they are harvested: the later in the season the syrup is harvested, the darker the color and deeper the flavor. I prefer Grade A dark amber or Grade B; they have the best flavor for baking purposes. Choose organic to avoid the chemicals used in the processing of conventional syrup.

Raw Honey Unheated and unprocessed, raw honey still contains all the phytonutrients and other good stuff the bees put in there. This natural sweetener is also antiviral and immunity boosting. Typically, light-colored honey has a more delicate flavor that's better suited to baking than more robust, dark-colored honeys. Buy Wholesome Sweeteners brand or, better yet, honey locally produced in your area.

Butter and Oil

The air bubbles that butter and other fats create in batter not only help cakes rise, but are responsible for the light and creamy texture of buttercream frosting. From a health perspective, the subject of fats can be confusing and controversial, but if you choose only fats from whole foods, you're good to go.

Butter Always use sweet and unsalted butter for baking, and make sure it is at room temperature. In fact, making sure that all your ingredients are at room temperature before you mix them is the single most important tip I can share with you for baking success. If a recipe calls for melted butter, cool it to room temperature before adding. The very best butter for baking is unsalted Kerrygold, an Irish butter made from grass-fed, hormone-free cow's milk. It has a high butterfat content, another factor that's extremely important to baking success: the fat provides the flavor, texture, and all-important air pockets. Whenever possible, choose organic butter.

Earth Balance Vegan Buttery Sticks This dairy-free alternative to butter is made from a blend of expeller-pressed oils and is the only acceptable butter substitute to use in baking—they're that effective! Be sure to buy the sticks—not the kind in the tub, which is for table use—and do *not* substitute margarine. In any form, under any name, margarine is not a real food!

Nonhydrogenated Vegetable Shortening For a dairy-free alternative to butter, I use Spectrum brand organic vegetable shortening in my buttercream. It provides a lovely, creamy texture but does not contribute any flavor, so the extracts or other flavorings used in the buttercream can shine through.

Nonstick Cooking Spray This is a supereasy, nonmessy way to lightly oil your cake pans. Use cooking spray in combination with parchment paper, and your cakes will never stick. I like Spectrum canola spray oil and Kelapo soy-free cold-pressed extra-virgin coconut oil pan spray; both are organic. To apply, lightly spray both the bottom and the sides of the pan. Be sure to hold the pan over the sink so you don't get spray on the floor—it's very slippery. For tips on oiling and lining pans, see page 172.

Virgin Coconut Oil I'm a huge proponent of coconut oil, both for its health benefits and for its baking applications. Use it to grease your pans, or as a vegan/dairy-free alternative to melted butter. The "coconuttiness" of this oil varies from brand to brand, but most will *not* lend

a coconut flavor to your cakes or buttercreams. I use Barlean's or Spectrum brands, but bargains can be found at stores like Trader Joe's and Costco. Just make sure the label specifies "virgin" and "organic."

To use coconut oil in baking, scoop approximately the quantity that you need, melt it in a saucepan over low heat, and then measure the precise amount called for in the recipe. But be sure to cool it to room temperature before you add it to your batter.

Milk and Dairy-Free Alternatives

I recommend using top-quality organic dairy-free alternatives for the same reason you should use the highest-quality organic milk, cream, and cream cheese: they'll result in cakes that not only taste better and have a finer texture but are also more health supportive. Coconut milk, cream, and yogurt most closely resemble cow's milk in texture and fat content, and I prefer them over all of the other dairy-free options. They are without a doubt the most important element in successful dairy-free baking. Discovering coconut products changed my life in the kitchen. Seriously!

Coconut Milk (Carton) You can substitute unsweetened soy milk, almond milk, or any dairy-free milk you choose, but I always use unsweetened So Delicious coconut milk from a carton in my cakes. The results are most comparable to cow's milk.

Coconut Milk (Canned) Canned coconut milk, as opposed to the coconut milk that comes from a carton, is a perfect dairy-free substitute for cream. If you haven't tried it, you may be shocked by how creamy and delicious it is. Make sure you shake the can before opening to evenly distribute the fat-containing "cream" and the coconut water. Always choose regular coconut milk—not lite! The fat content is crucial to baking success. I use Native Forest unsweetened organic coconut milk.

Cream Cheese For my cream cheese icings, you can swap in a nondairy cream cheese of your choice. But if you're staying away from soy, feel free to swap in vanilla buttercream flavored with lemon, vanilla, or maple syrup.

Dairy-Free Buttermilk To make an easy dairy-free substitute for buttermilk, combine 1 cup unsweetened coconut or almond milk (from a carton) with 1 tablespoon freshly squeezed lemon juice and let sit for 15 minutes at room temperature. Make it just before you intend to use it; it does not store well.

Yogurt When baking with yogurt, I use So Delicious dairy-free cultured coconut milk yogurt exclusively. The plain and vanilla flavors are perfect for cakes. I love its creamy texture and flavor. If dairy isn't an issue for you, choose Greek yogurt for my cakes. I like Stonyfield Oikos brand.

Eggs and Egg Substitutes

Organic, pastured eggs are far superior to factory-farmed eggs in both flavor and nutritional value. They're higher in valuable omega-3 fats and vitamins, and are lower in cholesterol and fat. Look for pastured eggs at Whole Foods Market, farmers' markets, and your local food co-op. All my recipes were tested using large eggs.

If you're avoiding or eliminating eggs, I recommend a simple homemade egg replacer made from flaxseed. It will work in most of my recipes that call for eggs, but to get the light and airy texture delivered by egg whites, you need the real thing. Flaxseed is readily available in the gluten-free section of many grocery stores, or at Whole Foods. Store it in an airtight container in the freezer to extend its short shelf life for up to two years.

Flax Egg Replacer

This simple egg substitute contains just two ingredients: flaxseed and water. To grind the flaxseed, use a mini food processor or a coffee grinder dedicated to the task. This recipe makes the equivalent of one large egg.

1 tablespoon ground flaxseed
3 tablespoons water

In a glass measuring cup, whisk together the ground flaxseed and water. Set aside for about 3 minutes, or until the mixture has thickened and become fluffy. Add the flax eggs to the wet ingredients in your recipe and mix well to combine. Flax egg replacer works best in cakes that call for four eggs or fewer and will yield very similar results to the "real" thing.

Chocolate, Cocoa Powder, and Cacao Powder

Chocolate is one of those ingredients that can absolutely make or break your cake, so spend a little extra for a premium brand. High-quality chocolate is loaded with flavor that will greatly enhance your baked goods—not to mention their health benefits. Look for a chocolate with at least 63 percent cacao content; the percentage of cacao will be noted on the front of any good-quality product. The higher the cacao content, the more flavorful, intense, and nutritious the product.

I primarily use dark and white chocolate chips in the recipes in this book. Please take note: chocolate chips aren't always gluten free, and if you're dairy free, know that some semisweet and even dark chocolate chips contain dairy. Most white chocolate chips include dairy, and I haven't had a favorable baking experience with any of the available dairy free brands. For gluten- and dairy-free options, see my brand recommendations below, or check package labels with care.

Chocolate Chips I prefer Guittard extra-dark chocolate chips for baking; their quality can't be beat and they are gluten and dairy free. The company also sells luscious gluten-free white chocolate chips. If you can't find them at your local supermarket, you can purchase them online (see Sources, page 204). Another gluten-, dairy-, and nut-free option is Enjoy Life chocolate chips.

Cocoa Powder Choose a cocoa powder that says "natural" on the label; the darker dutch-process cocoa has been treated with an alkali, which will affect the flavor of your cake. I recommend Hershey's natural cocoa powder because it's so widely available. Don't use Hershey's Special Dark (a mix of natural and dutched cocoas) in your buttercream unless you want your icing to be grayish. Ghirardelli and Scharffen Berger are two other excellent brands to look out for. Natural and dutched cocoas have different formulations and react differently to baking soda and baking powder. My recipes have been formulated for natural cocoa powder, not dutched.

Raw Organic Cacao Powder I use this magical powder every day in my smoothies to make them intensely chocolaty and highly nutritious! A superhealthy (but quite expensive) alternative to cocoa powder, this is the pure ground cacao bean, milled at low temperature to protect the nutrients and flavor. A Mayan superfood that has been used medicinally for thousands of years, raw cacao powder is rich in antioxidants and polyphenols, fiber, magnesium, potassium, and iron. Because it is pricey, I call for it only in the Nana Banana Snack Cake (page 8), where it provides depth and richness. I recommend Navitas Naturals brand (see Sources, page 204).

Nuts and Shredded Coconut

Nuts I recommend using organic nuts; conventional walnuts are particularly pesticide heavy. If you buy them in bulk, purchase them from a store that has a high turnover rate to ensure freshness. Because of their high fat content, nuts can become rancid quickly. To extend their shelf life, freeze them for up to nine to twelve months, depending on the nut.

TOASTING NUTS

When I call for a nut garnish, feel free to toast the nuts if you prefer. Toasting nuts really brings out their flavor. Toast nuts whole and let them cool before chopping.

Preheat the oven to 350°F. Spread the nuts on a parchment-lined baking sheet in a single layer. Bake in the center of the oven until you start to smell the aroma of the nuts (typically 6 to 10 minutes), and then immediately remove them from the oven and transfer to a plate or platter to cool so they don't continue cooking on the baking sheet. Toasted nuts can be stored in a resealable plastic bag in the freezer up to 6 months.

To toast hazelnuts, toast as directed above, and then transfer to a clean, dry kitchen towel and rub them until the skins come off.

Shredded Coconut Although I wasn't always a fan of coconut, I'm a true believer now—I discovered that it was artificial coconut flavor I found off-putting. Always choose unsweetened coconut. I use Bob's Red Mill shredded or flaked coconut, which is unsweetened and unsulfured (see Sources, page 204).

TOASTING SHREDDED OR CHIPPED COCONUT

Spread the coconut on a baking sheet in a single layer and place in a preheated 350°F oven for about 5 minutes or until the coconut begins to brown slightly and you can smell the aroma. When you open the oven door, stand back so you're not blasted with the essential oils from the coconut; they can irritate your eyes for a brief moment. Transfer the pan to a rack to cool completely before using, and then store the toasted coconut in an airtight container at room temperature up to 2 weeks.

Flavoring Extracts and Pastes

I use only pure vanilla and almond extracts and vanilla bean paste in my recipes. Nielsen-Massey brand is my favorite—there's just no comparison. Its cold-extraction process allows even the subtlest of vanilla's three hundred flavor compounds to shine through, and all of its vanillas are gluten, allergen, and GMO free. Same goes for Nielsen-Massey's almond extract, which is made from the purest oil of bitter almonds. This brand is becoming more widely available in stores, or you can purchase it online (see Sources, page 204).

Pure Vanilla Extract Imitation vanilla is just that, imitation—not *real* vanilla. It is composed *entirely* of artificial ingredients, including by-products from the paper industry like coal tar. Coal-tar-flavored cakes and buttercreams? No thanks! Pure vanilla is made by steeping real vanilla-bean pods in an alcohol-water solution in order to extract the vanilla's essential flavors. It is more expensive than imitation vanilla because vanilla beans are made by Mother Nature—not in a factory or laboratory—and they are difficult to cultivate. Pure vanilla extract will last indefinitely and it only improves with age.

Vanilla Bean Paste I have only recently begun to use this beautiful product in my baking—and I highly recommend that you order some right now! It combines the tiny seeds from the vanilla pod with pure vanilla extract to create a paste with a wonderful flavor and aroma; the seeds contribute lovely little brown specks to your crème anglaise or buttercream. Thanks to its thick consistency, which is similar to molasses, you can use this paste to add vanilla flavor to cake batters or sauces without thinning them out.

Vanilla Beans Vanilla extract and paste are ideal for batters and buttercreams, but the actual seeds from the vanilla-bean pod are perfect for crème anglaise and custard. Just slice the pod from end to end and open it to reveal the brown seeds. Using the tip of a paring knife, scrape the seeds from the pod and use them in your recipe. You can place the scraped pod in a canister of sugar to lend an aromatic vanilla essence to your sugar.

Pure Almond Extract As with vanilla extract, always choose real almond extract—never imitation. It's made from oil extracted from bitter almonds to deliver optimal flavor results. There is a huge difference in the flavor quality of various almond extracts. I recommend using Nielsen-Massey or Simply Organic brands for the best results (see page 204).

Coffee and Espresso Powder

Coffee I promise, adding coffee to your chocolate cake batter won't make your cake taste like coffee: coffee enhances chocolate, making its flavor more full, rounded, and rich. I use the same coffee I drink in the morning, an organic dark French roast, but you can use any good-quality drinking coffee.

Instant Espresso Powder Not to be confused with ground espresso beans, espresso powder is a very dark, strong instant coffee. I use Medaglia d'Oro brand, which can be found in the coffee aisle of some supermarkets or purchased online (see Sources, page 204). It's crucial in my Mocha Latte Cupcakes (page 80), which feature an espresso buttercream. And, in my Mocha Coffee Cake (page 18), it infuses all the components (espresso, streusel, and glaze) with rich coffee flavor.

Fruit

For natural fruit flavor, I use sliced peaches, apples, and pears, fruit purees, and an abundance of berries, citrus juices, and citrus zest. You can make my cakes that feature fruit any time of year, but recipes like Peaches and Cream Cake (page 44) and Pink Velvet Strawberry Cake (page 52) will be best when the fruits and berries are at their glorious seasonal peak. I've called for frozen berries when appropriate, as in some of my fruit purees; otherwise, I don't recommend subbing.

Citrus Juice and Zest It's important to look for organic citrus fruit whenever a recipe calls for zest. The zest comes from the outermost rind of the fruit, which is precisely where the majority of chemical residues from pesticides reside. Purchasing organic ensures a pesticide-free fruit. It's your call whether you also want to purchase organic fruit for the lemon, lime, and orange juices in my recipes, but for optimal flavor be sure to use freshly squeezed juice when I specify it.

Fruit Purees and Jams Choose a natural or an organic spread when possible, and look for purees and jams that use cane sugar as their sweetener. For flavor and your health, it is always better to choose a product that uses natural, minimally processed sugar over an artificial sweetener.

Whole Fruits and Berries I use organic fruits and berries in my cakes, but I understand that they are more expensive. If you want help prioritizing which organic items to buy, I recommend that you purchase organic berries and apples (these crops are treated heavily with pesticides and other chemicals). If you're baking with nonorganic apples, pears, or peaches, I recommend peeling them.

Other Gluten-Free Baking Essentials

Almond Meal or Flour This is simply blanched almonds that have been ground into a fine meal. For great flavor and texture, I use it in the Polenta Breakfast Cake (page 24) and in both the cake and the crumb topping of the Nana Banana Snack Cake (page 8). Almond meal is easy to make yourself—see the recipe in the sidebar. For store-bought, I recommend Bob's Red Mill almond meal; it's finely ground and gluten free.

MAKE YOUR OWN ALMOND MEAL

To make 1 cup of almond meal from scratch, simply pulse 1½ cups blanched almonds in a food processor or blender until very finely ground. Don't just turn on the processor and walk away, as you may return to discover you've made almond butter! Freeze leftovers in an airtight container up to 6 months.

Baking Powder and Soda Baking powder can be a source of hidden gluten. To leaven my cakes, I use Rumford aluminum-free baking powder, a gluten-free brand that's available at almost every supermarket. Baking soda is gluten free.

Cornstarch A fine powder made from corn kernels, cornstarch is used to thicken custards and puddings. I use it to thicken my pastry cream (page 166). Because cornstarch tends to form lumps, it is typically mixed with a small amount of a cold liquid or a granular solid like sugar, which helps disperse it. Not all cornstarch is gluten free, so check the label before purchasing. I use Bob's Red Mill brand; it's gluten free and made from corn that is not genetically modified.

Fine Sea Salt The purpose of adding salt to cake batter is not to create a salty flavor, but to enhance the other flavors in the cake. Choose fine sea salt for baking; its small grains will melt into the batter better than the coarser sea salt you may use for cooking. Sea salt is a natural product (the result of evaporating salt water) and is *far* superior to table salt, which is highly processed and contains additives.

Xanthan Gum Because gluten is the protein that holds traditional cakes together, you need to pair gluten-free flour blends with a binder; I use xanthan gum. Although its name sounds alien, xanthan gum is an all-natural powder that's readily available in the gluten-free sections of many supermarkets or online. I use Bob's Red Mill brand (see Sources, page 204).

Equipment

If you enjoy baking, you probably own most of the tools that you'll need. But if you're a newbie baker, here are some baking essentials you'll want to have at your fingertips, along with tips on how to use them properly that will be helpful regardless of your skill level. If you want to make the celebration cakes in chapter 5—and I highly recommend that you do—you'll need a handful of special tools; all are inexpensive and itemized under the ingredients list for each cake.

Appliances

Food Processor While not essential to make the recipes in this book, a food processor (or mini version) fitted with a metal blade attachment makes short order of chopping nuts. I also use it to make the cake crumbs that coat the sides of my Chocolate Orange Gâteaux (page 116). If you don't own one, you can make the crumbs in a blender, using an on-off motion, until they are finely ground.

Stand Mixer A regular handheld mixer can certainly do the job, but a heavy-duty stand mixer provides the most power and versatility. It comes with both a paddle attachment that you'll use to mix cake batters and buttercreams and a wire "whip" attachment that's just the thing for making whipped cream and meringues. Because you don't have to hold it up while it works, it saves your energy and leaves your hands free for adding ingredients. You can even walk away for a moment to get an ingredient from the fridge while the mixer keeps doing its thing. Be sure to regularly scrape down the bowl with a rubber spatula so that all of the ingredients get incorporated. I've reminded you to do so within the recipe instructions, just so you don't forget. Note: If you'll be using a handheld mixer, it may not be as powerful as a stand mixer. That's not a problem, just increase the mixing times in my instructions slightly if you see that your batter or icing hasn't achieved the state I describe.

Picks and Pans

The majority of these cakes can be made with the basics: 8-inch and 9-inch round cake pans, a cupcake pan, a 9 by 13-inch cakepan, and, of course, several wire cooling racks to ensure good air circulation after your cakes come out of the oven. Always choose metal versions—not glass. If you want to make all the cakes, there are a few other pans you'll need: a 10-inch-diameter Bundt pan, which has a hole through the middle and deeply fluted curves; a 10-inch-diameter tube pan with a hole in the middle and smooth sides; a 13 by 18-inch jelly-roll pan, which is simply a baking sheet with four low sides; and 3½-inch-diameter ramekins, individual porcelain baking dishes that are essential for making the Molten Chocolate Truffle Cakes (page 111). (Don't substitute a cupcake pan for ramekins because it distributes heat differently.)

All the recipes were tested with heavy-duty, light-colored metal pans, which help prevent overbrowning. If you have dark metal pans (or lightweight ones), they will absorb heat more quickly and your cakes and cupcakes may be done sooner than the bake times listed with each recipe. Set your kitchen timer for 10 minutes sooner than the lower range of the bake time (5 minutes for cupcakes) and do a toothpick test for doneness to ensure you don't overbake your cake.

Tools and Utensils

Couplers If you want to be able to change piping designs in the middle of decorating a cake, you'll need to use a coupler. They come in two parts, the cone-shaped piece that fits into the bag and the ring that screws on over the tip and cone to hold the tip in place. Couplers are inexpensive, so buy several—just like socks that go missing in the dryer, couplers have a way of disappearing. They come in small and large sizes, so if you plan on using small and large tips, you'll want both on hand. For piping techniques, see page 175.

Offset Spatula If you don't already own one, this is a key cake-decorating tool I recommend you buy. Although you can frost the cakes and cupcakes in this book without one, it's a great tool with many applications; the small size is perfect for icing cupcakes, and the larger size for cakes. They can also be used for lifting delicate items like cakelet rounds or modeling chocolate decor up and off your work surface. You can purchase them for as little as $6 or $7 in the decorating section of a hobby shop. Ones with wooden handles are my favorite.

Pastry Bags Disposable bags make for easy cleanup, but they aren't eco-friendly, so I use them only when working with dyed icings that will stain the white bags or when a very small scissor-snipped hole is required for drizzling (see page 182). Of the washable bag options, I prefer "featherweight" bags; they are thinner than their counterparts, making the whole setup less bulky in your hands. Bags come in many sizes, but I recommend that you start with 12-inch bags—any larger and they become unwieldy, any smaller and you have to refill them often.

Pastry Tips Of the dozens of tips available, I find myself using only a handful on a regular basis. With just four to six tips, you can create dozens of designs (see page 175). The basic shapes are round (a.k.a. plain), star, leaf, and petal. All come in small and large sizes, but I find that I only use both the small and the large ones for star designs; for round, leaf, and petal designs, I use small tips. Tips are numbered according to a standardized system: for a starter kit, I recommend that you purchase round #5, star #30, leaf #69, petal #104, and large star #1B.

Serrated Cake Knife If you want to split your cake layers in half to create four-layer cakes (see page 173 for instructions), you'll need a long-bladed serrated cake knife. Ateco and Fat Daddio's are two good brands; you shouldn't have to spend more than $20.

ALLERGEN-FREE *and* VEGAN CAKES CHART

I developed this cookbook so that all of you gluten-free folks can bake and enjoy your favorite cakes. But I'm well aware that an increasing number also have sensitivities to dairy, nuts, or soy, and the ranks of vegans who eschew all animal products are growing at a rapid pace. So I provided ingredient alternatives to address these needs wherever possible. The checklist below makes it easy for you to choose cake recipes that suit your dietary requirements.

Note: Although the FDA classifies coconut as a tree nut, it typically does not cause allergic reactions. Recipes that use coconut are marked Nut Free here. Don't despair if you see a recipe you'd love to make that doesn't match up with your needs: just swap out the problematic cake batter, filling, or frosting for one of the other recipes. You may just end up creating a cake that's better than the original rendition!

BREAKFAST, SNACK & COFFEE CAKES

	Dairy Free	Vegan	Nut Free	Soy Free
Nana Banana Snack Cake, page 8	x	x		x
Angel Food Cake with Fresh Berries, page 11	x		x	x
Buttermilk Bundt Cake with Peaches, page 12	x	x	x	x
Poppy Seed Bundt with Clementine Glaze, page 14	x	x	x	x
Lemon Blueberry Bundt with Glistening Lemon Glaze, page 16	x	x	x	x
Honey-Lavender Tea Cake, page 17	x	x	x	x
Mocha Coffee Cake, page 18	x	x		x
Apple-Cinnamon Coffee Cake with Almond Streusel, page 20	x	x		x
Pumpkin Spice Cake with Creamy Cinnamon Glaze, page 21	x	x	x	x
Polenta Breakfast Cake with Honey-Citrus Syrup, page 24	x	x		x
Pineapple Upside-Down Cake, page 25	x	x	x	x
Fruitcake with Citrus-Ginger Syrup, page 26	x	x		x
Gingerbread Cake with Fresh Ginger and Citrus Glaze, page 29	x	x	x	x

	Dairy Free	Vegan	Nut Free	Soy Free
Chocolate and Vanilla Marbled Cakes, page 30	x	x	x	x
Texas Sheet Cake, page 32	x	x	x	x

LAYER CAKES

	Dairy Free	Vegan	Nut Free	Soy Free
Triple Lemon Cake, page 38	x		x	x
Very Vanilla Cake with Fudgy Frosting, page 40	x		x	x
Peaches and Cream Cake, page 44	x		x	x
Hummingbird Cake with White Chocolate Cream Cheese Icing, page 47				x
Maple Walnut Cake with Cinnamon Maple Buttercream, page 50	x			x
Southern Coconut Cake, page 51	x		x	x
Pink Velvet Strawberry Cake with Strawberry Buttercream, page 52	x		x	x
German Chocolate Cake, page 55	x	x		x
Boston Cream Pie, page 56	x		x	x
Carrot Cake with Brown Sugar and Cinnamon Cream Cheese Icing, page 58	x	x		x
Cinnamon Spice Cake with Almond Buttercream, page 59	x			x
Caramel Cream Cake, page 60	x		x	x
Chocolate Layer Cake, page 63	x	x	x	x
Chocolate Peppermint Cake with Peppermint Buttercream, page 64	x	x	x	x

CUPCAKES FILLED & FROSTED

	Dairy Free	Vegan	Nut Free	Soy Free
Strawberry Shortcake Cupcakes, page 73	x		x	x
Banana Cream Cupcakes with Chocolate Ganache, page 74	x		x	x
Peanut Butter and Jelly Cupcakes, page 76	x			x
Chocolate Obsession Cupcakes, page 77	x	x	x	x
Salted Caramel and Apple Cupcakes, page 78	x		x	x
Mocha Latte Cupcakes, page 80	x	x	x	x
Ancho Chile, Chocolate, and Cinnamon Cupcakes, page 83	x	x	x	x

	Dairy Free	Vegan	Nut Free	Soy Free
Chocolate Hazelnut Cupcakes, page 86	x	x		x
Orange Chocolate Cheesecake Cupcakes, page 87	x		x	x
Pumpkin Ginger Cupcakes, page 88	x	x	x	x
Chocolate-Cherry Kirsch Cupcakes, page 91	x	x	x	x
Lemon Meringue Cupcakes, page 92	x		x	x
Margarita Lime Zingers, page 94	x		x	x

PLATED SLICES & LITTLE CAKES

	Dairy Free	Vegan	Nut Free	Soy Free
Chocolate Raspberry Ruffled Cakelets, page 100	x	x	x	x
Baked Alaska Bombes, page 103	x		x	x
Flourless Chocolate Torte with Cherry-Berry Puree, page 106	x	x	x	x
S'mores Cakes, page 108	x		x	x
Molten Chocolate Truffle Cakes, page 111	x		x	x
Cinnamon Mini Cakes with Caramelized Pears and Golden Sugar Halos, page 112	x		x	x
Chocolate Orange Gâteaux with Grand Marnier Crème Anglaise, page 116	x	x	x	x
White and Dark Chocolate Checkerboard Cake, page 119			x	x
Chocolate-Glazed Raspberry-Vanilla Jelly Roll with Chambord Crème Anglaise, page 112	x		x	x

DECORATED SPECIAL-OCCASION CAKES

	Dairy Free	Vegan	Nut Free	Soy Free
Pretty as a Package Cake, page 128	x	x	x	x
Wild at Heart Cake, page 132	x		x	x
Pink Princess Cake, page 134	x		x	x
Camo Cake, page 138	x	x	x	x
Two-Tiered Whimsy Cake, page 143	x		x	x
Fright Night Mummy Cake, page 146	x	x	x	x
White Christmas Bûche de Noël, page 148	x		x	x

SOURCES

Here's where you can find the gluten-free (and dairy-free) ingredients used in the recipes in this book, plus the baking and decorating equipment and tools I recommend in "Your Gluten-Free Baking Pantry" (page 188) and chapter 5. Many of the ingredients also can be found at Whole Foods Market or another natural foods supermarket chain—or at your local health foods store. These days, many supermarkets feature extensive gluten-free sections, too (yippee!).

GENERAL

Amazon
amazon.com

I've been shopping on Amazon for baking ingredients and equipment for years and it continually amazes me with its vast selection. You can find just about every ingredient you need to make the recipes in this book, as well as baking pans, tools, and decorating equipment. Fat Daddio's cake pans, baking sheets, and jelly-roll pans; Ateco pastry bags and tips; and ramekins, offset spatulas, and more can all be found here at great prices. In fact, Amazon generally has the best prices available anywhere and offers many items in bulk for further savings.

Country Kitchen Sweet Art
countrykitchensa.com

If you have a passion for the cake arts, consider this your go-to store; it has absolutely everything under the sun for cake decorating, baking, and sugar craft. I sourced products from Country Kitchen for Sublime Bakery and use it for my personal baking needs, so I can vouch for its extensive selection and excellent customer service.

Williams-Sonoma
williams-sonoma.com

A reliable source for high-quality baking appliances and gadgets (including the kitchen blowtorches I'm so fond of), this nationwide kitchen supply retailer also sells select baking ingredients, including the Cup4Cup gluten-free flour blend mentioned on page 190, and Nielsen-Massey's pure vanilla extract and paste recommended for all the recipes in this book. Order from the company's website or visit a store near you.

CHOCOLATE AND CACAO

Enjoy Life
enjoylifefoods.com

These gluten-, dairy-, and nut-free chocolate chips are available at Whole Foods and some Target, Kroger, and Safeway stores, or online from the company's site or Amazon.

Guittard Chocolate Company
guittard.com

This artisanal chocolate company sells top-quality gluten-free white chocolate chips and gluten-free, dairy-free extra-dark chocolate chips. Find them online at the company's site or Amazon.

Navitas Naturals
navitasnaturals.com

Navitas makes raw organic cacao powder and organic coconut palm sugar that is available at Whole Foods, Sprouts, Vitamin Shoppe, or online from the company's site or Amazon.

COCONUT OIL AND PAN SPRAYS

Kelapo
kelapo.com

Kelapo's soy-free organic extra-virgin coconut oil pan spray is available at Whole Foods, or online from the company's site or Amazon.

Spectrum Organics
spectrumorganics.com

Spectrum makes organic pan spray, vegan shortening, and virgin coconut oil that are sold at some Target and Kroger stores, or online at Amazon and Vitacost.com (or see the company's store locator on its website).

DAIRY AND DAIRY-FREE ALTERNATIVES

Earth Balance
earthbalancenatural.com

You can find Earth Balance Vegan Buttery Sticks, a natural, dairy-free alternative, at Whole Foods, health foods stores, and many grocery stores.

Kerrygold Pure Irish Butter
kerrygoldusa.com

This is all-natural unsalted butter from grass-fed cows. Find it at many grocery stores (see the store locator on the company's site) or online at Amazon.

So Delicious Dairy Free
sodeliciousdairyfree.com

So Delicious makes unsweetened coconut milk (in a carton) and cultured coconut milk yogurt, available at Whole Foods and at some Safeway, Kroger, and HEB stores.

ESPRESSO POWDER

Medaglia D'Oro
medagliadoro.com

This is top-quality instant espresso powder for your baking needs, available at some grocery stores and online at Amazon and Javacabana.com.

FLOURS AND BAKING SODA

Arrowhead Mills
arrowheadmills.com

This organic baking company makes a range of gluten-free flours, including white rice flour. See the company's store locator to find a store near you, or order online at Amazon.

Bob's Red Mill
bobsredmill.com

Bob's Red Mill offers an extraordinary selection of gluten-free flours, including hard-to-find bean and nut flours. You'll also find the tapioca starch, potato starch, cornstarch, xanthan gum, and shredded coconut that I use in these recipes. This employee-owned company has been offering gluten-free products for more than thirty years. The brand is widely available in the gluten-free section of grocery stores. See the store locator on the company's website to find a retailer near you, or order online from the site.

Cup4Cup
cup4cup.com

Although I recommend that you use homemade flour blends (page 191), Cup4Cup is a gluten-free all-purpose flour blend that I like. For instructions on swapping it in, see page 190. It's available at Williams-Sonoma and Whole Foods, or check the company's site to find other retailers near you that carry this product.

Mama's Almond Blend All-Purpose Gluten-Free Flour
glutenfreemama.com

This flour does not contain any leaveners, which makes it a possible substitute for homemade flour blends. Unlike the Cup4Cup flour blend, which contains some milk powder, it is also dairy-free/vegan. Use the store finder at the company's website to find a store near you, or purchase the flour directly from the company's site.

Rumford/Clabber Girl

clabbergirl.com

This aluminum-free baking powder is widely available at grocery stores, or online from the company's site or Amazon.

FRUIT SPREADS

Crofter's

croftersorganic.com

Crofter's two dozen exquisitely crafted fruit spreads are all USDA Certified Organic, Non-GMO Project Verified, and Fairtrade. Use the store finder online at the company's site to find a store near you, or purchase online at Amazon.

GRAHAM CRACKERS

Kinnikinnick Foods

kinnikinnick.com

These gluten-free graham crackers are available at Whole Foods or online at the company's site or Amazon.

HERBS AND SPICES

Frontier Natural Products Co-op

frontiercoop.com

This website offers a wide selection of organic, nonirradiated, Fairtrade herbs and spices, including Simply Organic, Aura Cacia, and Frontier's own products.

The Spice House

thespicehouse.com

This is my source for food-grade lavender flower buds.

Sur La Table

surlatable.com

Pure lavender extract is available at the company's stores or online.

SWEETENERS

Wholesome Sweeteners

wholesomesweeteners.com

This is your one-stop shop for organic sweeteners, including cane sugar, coconut palm sugar, and raw honey. Their products are Fairtrade certified, organic, natural, and Non-GMO Project Verified. Available at Whole Foods, Costco, Kroger, Sprouts, Wegman's, and HEB, or online from the company's site.

VANILLA AND OTHER EXTRACTS

Flavorganics

flavorganics.com

Shop for organic extracts, including coconut, almond, peppermint, and vanilla online at the company's website or Amazon.

Nielsen-Massey Fine Vanillas and Flavors

nielsenmassey.com

Nielsen-Massey makes incomparable pure vanilla extract and vanilla bean paste, available at Williams-Sonoma stores or online and from Amazon. (Or check out the company's "where to buy" information on its site.)

Olive Nation

olivenation.com

Despite the name, Olive Nation makes a wide variety of pure extracts, including alcohol-free vanilla. Shop online at its website or at Amazon.

Simply Organic

simplyorganic.com

Simply Organic makes organic almond, peppermint, and vanilla extracts. Use its store locator to find a source, or purchase online at the website or Amazon.

ACKNOWLEDGMENTS

———

Writing a cookbook is a labor of love, one that cannot be accomplished alone. I'm thankful for the many people who have supported me over the years and worked alongside me these past months.

To my mother, thank you for giving me *The Betty Crocker Cookbook for Kids* when I was nine, and for always believing in my dreams.

Thank you to Sharon, my gal-pal and "cricket," for being by my side through thick and thin. There's never been a truer friend than you.

To Cade, my son and official recipe taster, thank you for your love, support, inspiration, and humor.

To Michel Nischan, you plucked a home baker from obscurity and turned her into a pastry chef. You saw greatness in me even before I could glimpse it myself. Thank you, Miche.

Thank you to Ragnhild Bakke and Even Andreas Bakke, for inspiring me to pursue my culinary passions instead of playing it safe.

To the great Julia Child, thank you for your kind and encouraging words so many years ago. Our brief meeting lit a fire in me that still burns to this day.

Thank you to my agent, Stephany Evans, for your belief in me and for finding my book a good home.

To Sarah, my co-writer, I never would have survived this task without you. Your skill and experience have been invaluable.

To my amazing team at Ten Speed Press, thank you for putting my ideas and creations together in a beautiful and useful book. To Julie Bennett, for welcoming my project on board. To Ali Slagle, for wrangling my words and recipes into a cohesive and well-thought-out book, and to Hannah Rahill, for championing this project. To Abigail Bok and Karen Levy, for your precision. Thank you to my publicist, Kara Van de Water. To the brilliant creative team of Erin Kunkel, Emma Campion, and Robyn Valarik for bringing my recipes to life with beautiful photos that perfectly capture my style and aesthetic. To Sarah Adelman, for bringing it all together so magnificently.

Lastly, and most of all, to my dad, my Sweetie Peach. Your example has inspired me to always reach for the stars, shoot for the moon, and soar with eagles.

Thank you.

ABOUT *the* AUTHORS

CATHERINE "CAT" RUEHLE Catherine "Cat" Ruehle is a renowned pastry chef, television personality, cake-decorating teacher, and holistic health coach who has made it her mission to give everyone's favorite sweet treats a healthy, gluten-free (and delicious!) makeover. *The New York Times* called her desserts at Michel Nischan's Miche Mache "breathtaking in both artistry and taste," and she and her cakes have made appearances on WE Network's *Get Married* and *Whose Wedding Is It Anyway?*, as well as Style Network's *My Fair Wedding* with David Tutera. In 2010, she became a regular competitor on *Food Network Challenge*, dazzling viewers with her over-the-top cakes.

A painful and crippling autoimmune disease struck Cat at the end of 2010, threatening to end her culinary career. Instead of turning to a lifetime of toxic medications, she overhauled her lifestyle by removing food triggers like gluten and dairy from her diet. Determined to help others overcome health challenges through food, she received nutrition training from the Institute for Integrative

Nutrition and launched a new business, A Well-Nourished Life, which offers holistic health consulting services to clients all over the United States. She lives in Fort Worth, Texas. Connect with Cat online at catruehle.com.

SARAH SCHEFFEL is an editor and writer specializing in cooking and health. Over the past 20 years, she has been involved in every aspect of cookbook creation from developmental editing and book packaging to writing and recipe testing. Recent titles include *The Baker's Book of Essential Recipes* and *Easy Gluten-Free!* for *Good Housekeeping*.

She is a graduate of the chefs' training program at the Natural Gourmet Institute for Health and Culinary Arts, where she studied health-supportive cooking and vegan and gluten-free diets. She divides her time between Brooklyn and Woodstock, New York.

INDEX

___

All rights reserved.
Published in the United States by Ten Speed Press, an imprint of the
Crown Publishing Group, a division of Random House LLC,
a Penguin Random House Company, New York.
www.crownpublishing.com
www.tenspeed.com

Ten Speed Press and the Ten Speed Press colophon
are registered trademarks of Random House LLC

Library of Congress Cataloging-in-Publication Data

Ruehle, Catherine.
  Let us all eat cake : gluten-free recipes
for everyone's favorite cakes /
Catherine Ruehle with Sarah Scheffel.
    pages cm
1. Gluten-free diet—Recipes. 2. Baking. 3. Cake.
I. Scheffel, Sarah. II. Title.
  RM237.86.R84 2014
  641.81'5—dc23

              2013049695

Hardcover ISBN: 978-1-60774-629-4
eBook ISBN: 978-1-60774-630-0

Printed in China

Design by Sarah Adelman
Food styling by Robyn Valarik
Author photograph by Craftsy

10 9 8 7 6 5 4 3 2 1

First Edition

MEASUREMENT CONVERSION CHARTS

Volume

U.S.	IMPERIAL	METRIC
1 tablespoon	½ fl oz	15 ml
2 tablespoons	1 fl oz	30 ml
¼ cup	2 fl oz	60 ml
⅓ cup	3 fl oz	90 ml
½ cup	4 fl oz	120 ml
⅔ cup	5 fl oz (¼ pint)	150 ml
¾ cup	6 fl oz	180 ml
1 cup	8 fl oz (⅓ pint)	240 ml
1¼ cups	10 fl oz (½ pint)	300 ml
2 cups (1 pint)	16 fl oz (⅔ pint)	480 ml
2½ cups	20 fl oz (1 pint)	600 ml
1 quart	32 fl oz (1⅔ pints)	1 l

Temperature

FAHRENHEIT	CELSIUS/GAS MARK
250°F	120°C/gas mark ½
275°F	135°C/gas mark 1
300°F	150°C/gas mark 2
325°F	160°C/gas mark 3
350°F	180 or 175°C/gas mark 4
375°F	190°C/gas mark 5
400°F	200°C/gas mark 6
425°F	220°C/gas mark 7
450°F	230°C/gas mark 8
475°F	245°C/gas mark 9
500°F	260°C

Length

INCH	METRIC
¼ inch	6 mm
½ inch	1.25 cm
¾ inch	2 cm
1 inch	2.5 cm
6 inches (½ foot)	15 cm
12 inches (1 foot)	30 cm

Weight

U.S./IMPERIAL	METRIC
½ oz	15 g
1 oz	30 g
2 oz	60 g
¼ lb	115 g
⅓ lb	150 g
½ lb	225 g
¾ lb	350 g
1 lb	450 g